The Big
BOOK of
BLING

RITZY ROCKS, EXTRAVAGANT ANIMALS, SPARKLING SCIENCE, AND MORE!

Rose Davidson

NATIONAL GEOGRAPHIC
WASHINGTON, D.C.

CONTENTS

Interior of Marble House, one of the most famous mansions in Newport, Rhode Island, U.S.A.

Peacock mantis shrimp

Hope Diamond

BLING! When you hear that word, do you think of giant gems or gorgeous jewels? Or is it piles of money, diamond-encrusted cupcakes ... maybe even gold toilets?

While bling is certainly everything flashy, glittery, and rich, there's actually so much more to it than just shiny stuff. So, what is bling, really?

Say the word out loud and you might swear you can hear light striking the surface of a sparkling diamond. Linguists call a word that conjures up the idea of a sound an "ideophone." But only in recent decades did people start using the term "bling." Television ads and music videos use it to describe fancy, over-the-top accessories like extravagant watches and glistening gold necklaces. Just like a catchy tune, once "bling" got into our brains, it stuck around.

The truth is, though, bling isn't just for people with big bucks. Bling is all around us—whether it's an animal that amazes, a stone that sparkles, gear that glitters, or science that shimmers. And as long as you find beauty and value in something, it's as good as gold.

So, turn the pages and uncover the jaw-dropping secrets behind our world's most brilliant bling. Explore the wonders of nature by indulging in views of gorgeous glowing caves and shining lakes. Get ready to be astonished by animals that seem to trick the human eye with their crazy colors or surprising sheen. Unearth radiant rocks and magnificent minerals, lush landscapes, and majestic marvels. Take a step back in time to find sprawling kingdoms, royal relics, and reclaimed riches. And, yes, you'll even find some flashy fashion and other super splurges that might make you see dollar signs!

Prepare your eyes for the super sparkly, awesomely astonishing, and unbelievably opulent. You might be surprised by the world of wealth you discover.

Armor of Henry II, king of France

Tropical piranha

RiTZY
ROCKS

Glimmering rocks add glitz to just about anything: Dazzling diamonds and other gemstones summon *oohs* and *aahs* on necklaces and bracelets, while sparkling stones ignited prehistoric fires. We use other rocks in our everyday lives—and we even eat some! Whether they hold sinister secrets or capture the world's attention for their regal status, this bling has solid star power.

BIRTHSTONE MYTHS AND FACTS

Legends have long swirled about the powers of these precious stones. Separate the myths from the facts about your birth-month bling.

FEBRUARY: AMETHYST

Old-School Myths: Amethysts supposedly helped those who carried them stay awake and think clearly, protected against evil spells, and brought victory in battle.

Rock-Solid Facts: Amethysts are a kind of quartz commonly found in geodes. Sparkling raw amethyst crystals range in color from light mauve to deep purple. At one time, you could wear amethyst jewelry only if you were royalty.

JANUARY: GARNET

Old-School Myths: People once believed that garnets offered protection from poisons, wounds, and even scary dreams.

Rock-Solid Facts: You can find garnets in streams where water has worn away rock, exposing the gems. Before they're polished, garnets look like small pebbles. They come in shades of red, black, and green (the rarest). Some are even colorless.

MARCH: AQUAMARINE

Old-School Myths: People used to believe that aquamarines could protect sailors and their ships from disasters at sea. The aquamarine was also thought to heal illnesses that affected the stomach, liver, jaws, and throat—and was supposedly an antidote to poison, too.

Rock-Solid Facts: Aquamarines, which are a form of the mineral beryl, range from blue-green to deep blue. Naturally occurring deep-blue aquamarines are the rarest and most valuable. Some of these crystals weigh more than 250 pounds (113 kg)!

APRIL: DIAMOND >>>>

Old-School Myths: People associated the sparkle of diamonds with romance, mystery, power, greed, and magic. Many once believed that diamonds were made by bolts of lightning.

Rock-Solid Facts: Diamonds develop deep in the ground under great pressure. The gems are the crystalline form of carbon. (Another form of carbon is graphite, the "lead" in your pencil.) Diamonds are the hardest naturally occurring substance on Earth.

<< MAY: EMERALD

Old-School Myths: An emerald can melt a snake's eyes! Well, that's what people used to believe. They also thought these gems would relax your eyes if you looked through them. Other beliefs: Emeralds stopped bleeding, cured fevers, kept the wearer calm, and could even predict the future.

Rock-Solid Facts: Like aquamarines, emeralds are a form of the mineral beryl. These gems, often found in Colombia, South America, are light to deep green. Prized for its deep green color and clarity, the 37.8-carat Chalk Emerald—once the centerpiece to a necklace supposedly owned by Indian royalty—ranks as one of the world's finest emeralds.

JUNE: PEARL >>>>

Old-School Myths: Pearls were once thought to possess magical qualities. By law, only powerful, rich people could own and don the gemstones. According to legend, wealthy Roman women wore pearls to bed so that when they woke in the morning, they instantly remembered how rich they were.

Rock-Solid Facts: This is the only birthstone made by living creatures—oysters and other mollusks. Like other gems, pearls can be different colors, including white, black, blue, green, peach, and chocolate brown. The color of the mollusk's outer shell influences the pearl's color.

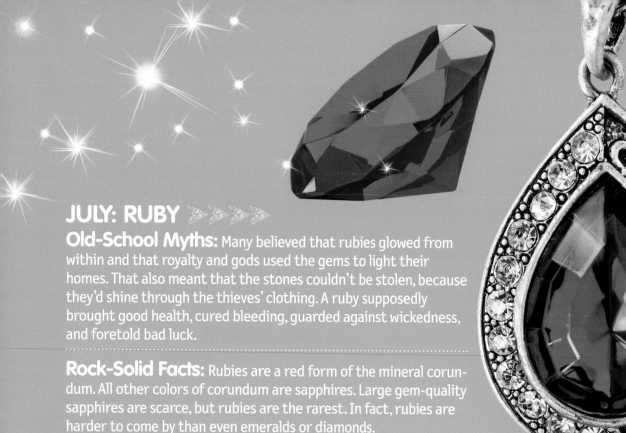

JULY: RUBY ▶▶▶

Old-School Myths: Many believed that rubies glowed from within and that royalty and gods used the gems to light their homes. That also meant that the stones couldn't be stolen, because they'd shine through the thieves' clothing. A ruby supposedly brought good health, cured bleeding, guarded against wickedness, and foretold bad luck.

Rock-Solid Facts: Rubies are a red form of the mineral corundum. All other colors of corundum are sapphires. Large gem-quality sapphires are scarce, but rubies are the rarest. In fact, rubies are harder to come by than even emeralds or diamonds.

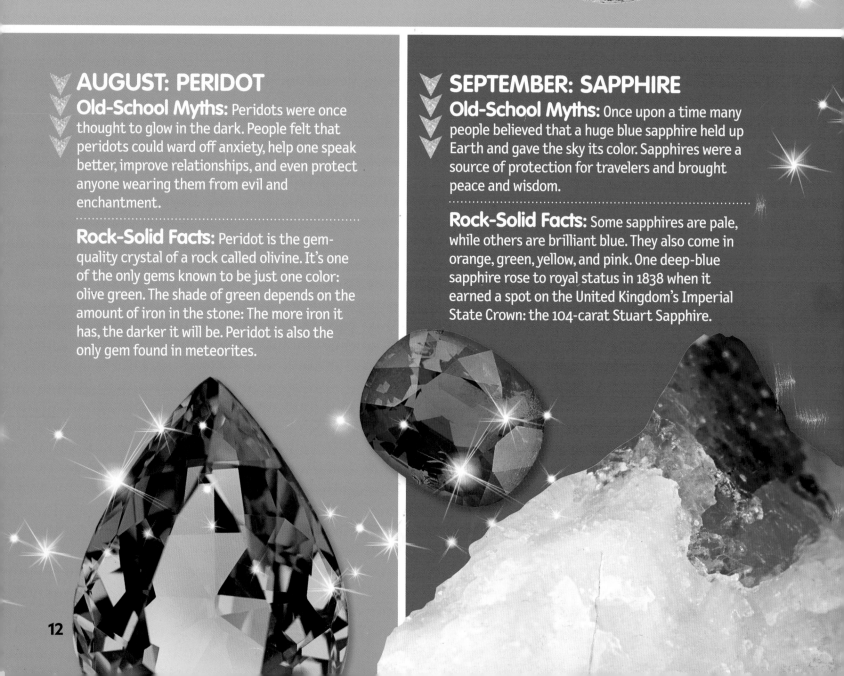

AUGUST: PERIDOT

Old-School Myths: Peridots were once thought to glow in the dark. People felt that peridots could ward off anxiety, help one speak better, improve relationships, and even protect anyone wearing them from evil and enchantment.

Rock-Solid Facts: Peridot is the gem-quality crystal of a rock called olivine. It's one of the only gems known to be just one color: olive green. The shade of green depends on the amount of iron in the stone: The more iron it has, the darker it will be. Peridot is also the only gem found in meteorites.

SEPTEMBER: SAPPHIRE

Old-School Myths: Once upon a time many people believed that a huge blue sapphire held up Earth and gave the sky its color. Sapphires were a source of protection for travelers and brought peace and wisdom.

Rock-Solid Facts: Some sapphires are pale, while others are brilliant blue. They also come in orange, green, yellow, and pink. One deep-blue sapphire rose to royal status in 1838 when it earned a spot on the United Kingdom's Imperial State Crown: the 104-carat Stuart Sapphire.

12

OCTOBER: OPAL

Old-School Myths: Wearing an opal will make you invisible—according to legend. An opal was also believed to bring beauty, success, and happiness, as well as medicinal powers to ward off heart and kidney failure. It was once said that an opal could even protect a person from lightning.

Rock-Solid Facts: Opals form over millions of years where hot, mineral-rich ooze—including the mineral silica—seeps into rock cracks. Tiny spheres of silica stack up and harden to become opals. The way light bounces off the silica creates an opal's colorful shimmer.

DECEMBER: TURQUOISE >>>>

Old-School Myths: Some people believed turquoise was a love charm. If a man gave a woman turquoise jewelry, he was pledging his love for her. Many Native Americans thought turquoise could bring rain during times of drought and ensured accurate aim while hunting. Even today in certain Native American cultures, the blue of turquoise symbolizes the sky and the green symbolizes Earth.

Rock-Solid Facts: Turquoise forms where mineral-rich water seeps into rocky gaps. Over time only the minerals remain—as turquoise. The copper in turquoise gives the gem its shades of blue and green.

NOVEMBER: TOPAZ

Old-School Myths: In ancient Egypt, the topaz's golden glow was said to come from the sun god Ra, and the stone was supposedly a powerful amulet against harm. Other legends proclaimed that a topaz cleared people's thinking, increased strength, and warned of poisoned food or drink. It supposedly cured insomnia and asthma, and stopped bleeding.

Rock-Solid Facts: Topazes come in a range of colors. Many of them are golden; some are pink, green, or colorless. There's some debate over the origin of the stone's name: Some say it's named after an island in the Red Sea, formerly called Topazios. Others say topaz gets its name from the Sanskrit word *tapas*, which means "fire."

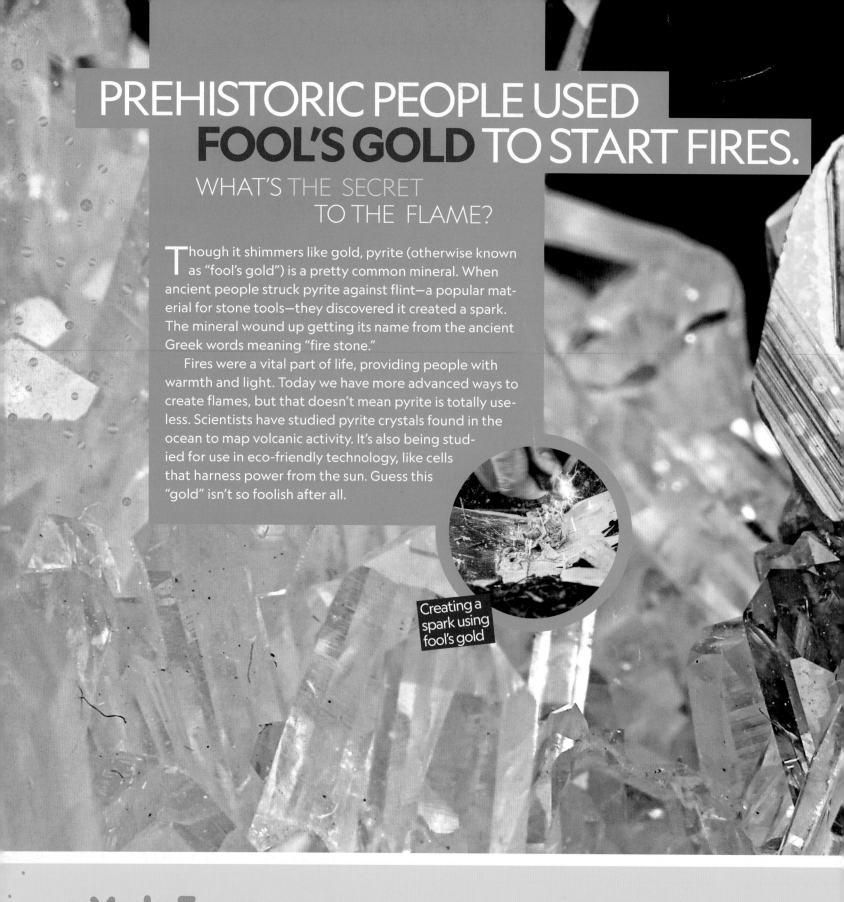

PREHISTORIC PEOPLE USED FOOL'S GOLD TO START FIRES.

WHAT'S THE SECRET TO THE FLAME?

Though it shimmers like gold, pyrite (otherwise known as "fool's gold") is a pretty common mineral. When ancient people struck pyrite against flint—a popular material for stone tools—they discovered it created a spark. The mineral wound up getting its name from the ancient Greek words meaning "fire stone."

Fires were a vital part of life, providing people with warmth and light. Today we have more advanced ways to create flames, but that doesn't mean pyrite is totally useless. Scientists have studied pyrite crystals found in the ocean to map volcanic activity. It's also being studied for use in eco-friendly technology, like cells that harness power from the sun. Guess this "gold" isn't so foolish after all.

Creating a spark using fool's gold

PYRITE VS. GOLD >
What's the DIFFERENCE?

Gold

WEIGHT
Gold is much heavier than pyrite.

Pyrite

◀ COLOR
Gold is a warmer tone of yellow. Pyrite looks more metallic.

Pyrite

◀ SHINE
Gold doesn't tarnish or lose its luster. Pyrite can tarnish, making it less shiny.

Gold
Pyrite

◀ SHAPE
Gold is often found in nuggets or flakes. Pyrite usually forms in cubes.

Gorgeous GEODES

To an untrained eye, an unopened geode looks like just your average rock. But waiting inside is a crystal wonderland. Within their mineral-lined cavities, geodes offer up a sparkling spectacle.

1

Geodes begin to form because of cavities, or holes, in rocks.

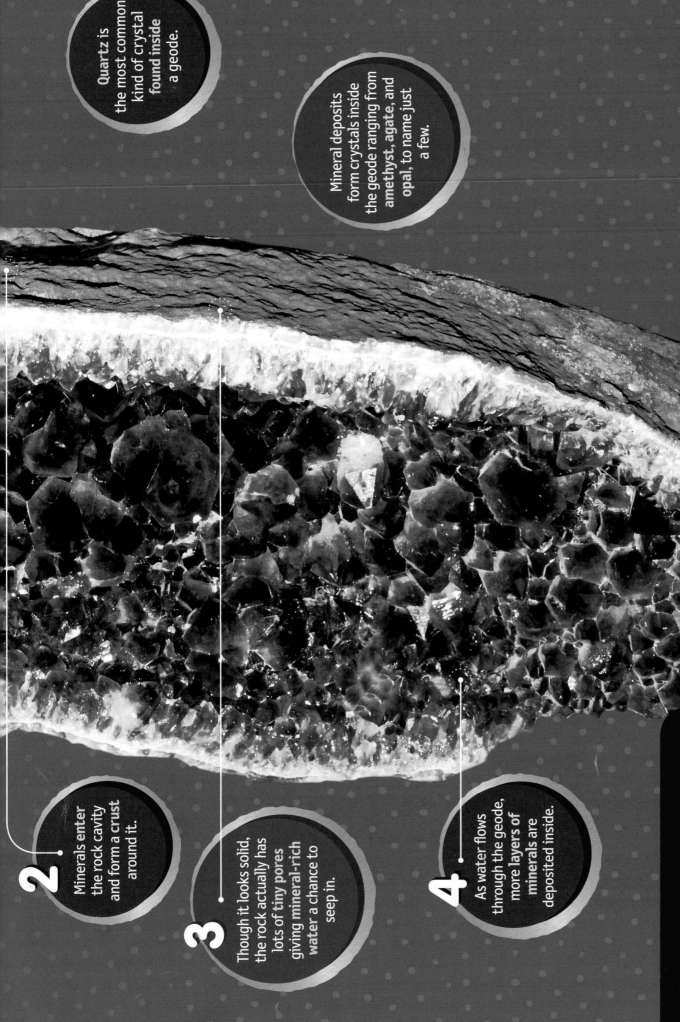

Quartz is the most common kind of crystal found inside a geode.

Mineral deposits form crystals inside the geode ranging from amethyst, agate, and opal, to name just a few.

2 Minerals enter the rock cavity and form a crust around it.

3 Though it looks solid, the rock actually has lots of tiny pores giving mineral-rich water a chance to seep in.

4 As water flows through the geode, more layers of minerals are deposited inside.

HOW TO SPOT A GEODE

PICK THE PLACE: Know where you're most likely to find a geode. Lakes, riverbeds, deserts, or other areas with lots of limestone or dry land are great places to search.

KEEP AN EYE OUT FOR EGGS: Geodes are usually round, often egg-shaped. If you see a rock with sharp edges, it's probably not a geode.

SKIP THE SMOOTH STONES: A geode's texture is lumpy, sometimes compared to a head of cauliflower.

COMPARE WEIGHT: Think you've found a winner? Locate a rock with a similar size and hold each one. If the candidate you've found is the real deal, it'll be lighter.

Crown
JEWELS

These toppers **TOTALLY RULE!**
Discover fantastic facts about
COOL CROWNS
from around the world.

ADDED UP, ALL THE ITEMS IN BRITAIN'S CROWN JEWELS COLLECTION ARE BEDAZZLED WITH 23,578 GEMS.

CROWN OF KOREA

Dangling gold disks and jade *gogoks* (comma-shaped beads) adorn this fifth-century headpiece from the Silla Kingdom, which once ruled the Korean Peninsula. Unearthed among a collection of treasures during the excavation of the king and queen's tomb, the crown is topped with five tall prongs representing trees and antlers.

BRITISH GLITZ

Bedazzled with 2,868 diamonds, 269 pearls, 17 sapphires, and 11 emeralds, the United Kingdom's Imperial State Crown is all glitz—mixed with a precarious past. Several famous gems have taken up residence on the regal headpiece, including the supposedly cursed Koh-i-Noor diamond. The crown weighs a whopping 2.3 pounds (1 kg)—that's like wearing seven baseballs on your head!

BOHEMIAN BLING

Studded with emeralds, sapphires, spinels, and pearls—along with a single ruby, rubellite, and aquamarine—the gem-encrusted Crown of St. Wenceslas hails from the Kingdom of Bohemia, which once reigned over part of the present-day Czech Republic in Europe. It's secured in Prague Castle behind seven different locks, each of which can only be opened by a key belonging to a different keeper. You could say they're keeping a tight lid on this crown.

> SPINELS ARE COLORFUL GEMSTONES THAT WERE OFTEN CONFUSED WITH RUBIES OR SAPPHIRES FOR MORE THAN 1,000 YEARS.

FAN OF IRAN

Worn by reigning members of a former Iranian dynasty, the red-velvet Kiani Crown is encrusted with 1,800 pearls, 300 emeralds, 1,800 rubies and spinels, and an unknown number of diamonds. The feathery-looking part of the topper, called an aigrette, can be removed from the headpiece by its butterfly-shaped base—in case the wearer needs to "dress down."

RUSSIAN RED

Crafted by a skilled jeweler, Russia's Great Imperial Crown was first used in the coronation of Catherine II, also known as Catherine the Great, in 1762. The crown dazzled with 4,936 diamonds, lines of pearls on either side of the exposed center, and a roughly 400-carat red spinel perched on top.

SALT, THE **ONLY ROCK THAT PEOPLE EAT,** WAS ONCE WORTH AS MUCH AS **GOLD.**

WHAT MAKES THIS SPLENDID SUBSTANCE SO HIGHLY PRIZED?

Before shakers of the crystal grains were commonplace on every dinner table, salt was considered a valuable form of currency throughout the world. It could be used for everything from preserving food to fighting off infections. The ancient Romans also used salt as payment for soldiers, which is likely where we get the word "salary," the regular amount someone gets paid for a job. It was so highly valued that, in the sixth century, merchants in Africa considered salt to be worth its weight in gold—literally! The merchants were known to trade an ounce of gold for an ounce of the prized mineral.

Merchants unload salt from a ship.

More
EVERYDAY MINERALS

FLUORITE
Thought to combat tooth decay, it's a common ingredient in toothpaste.

FELDSPAR
Many pottery glazes use this mineral to create shine.

CORUNDUM
This mineral makes rubies and sapphires, but it also reduces friction inside watches.

GYPSUM
This calcium-rich mineral is used as a baking aid in cakes.

MIMETITE

Found in lead deposits, this mineral contains arsenic—a naturally occurring element that, when consumed in high quantities, can be poisonous. It often forms glob-shaped crystals.

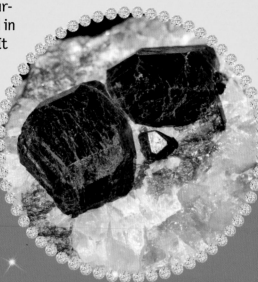

UVAROVITE

Though it looks like an emerald, this stone is actually a rare type of garnet. Most gemstone-quality deposits of uvarovite are found in Russia's Ural Mountains.

ODD

RHODOCHROSITE

This mineral's striking color makes it a popular pick for jewelry makers. However, its soft nature means it can't handle a lot of wear and tear. Earrings and necklaces are more common than rings for showcasing this stone.

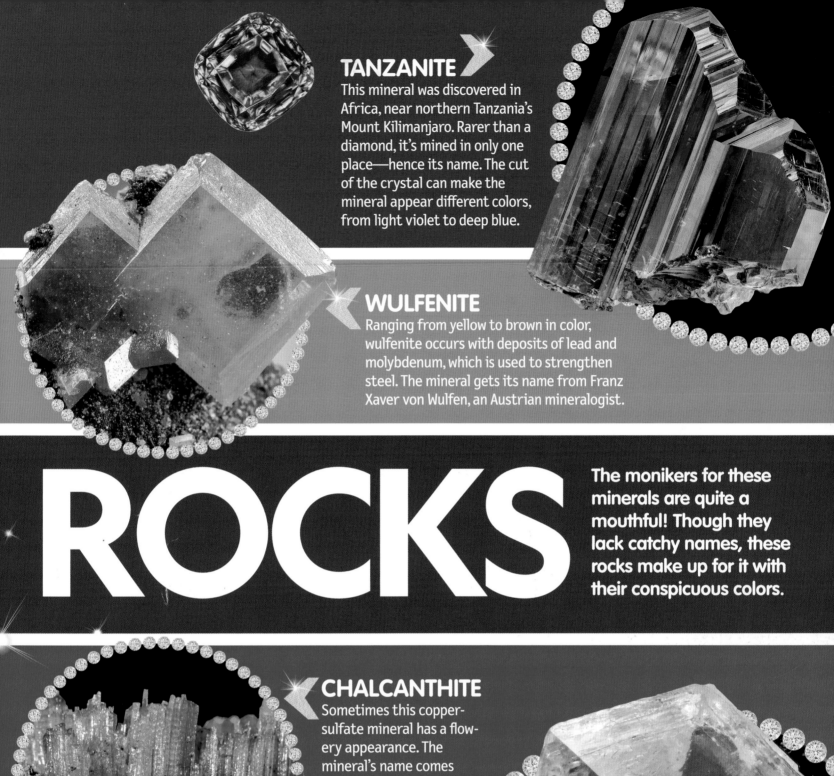

TANZANITE

This mineral was discovered in Africa, near northern Tanzania's Mount Kilimanjaro. Rarer than a diamond, it's mined in only one place—hence its name. The cut of the crystal can make the mineral appear different colors, from light violet to deep blue.

WULFENITE

Ranging from yellow to brown in color, wulfenite occurs with deposits of lead and molybdenum, which is used to strengthen steel. The mineral gets its name from Franz Xaver von Wulfen, an Austrian mineralogist.

ROCKS

The monikers for these minerals are quite a mouthful! Though they lack catchy names, these rocks make up for it with their conspicuous colors.

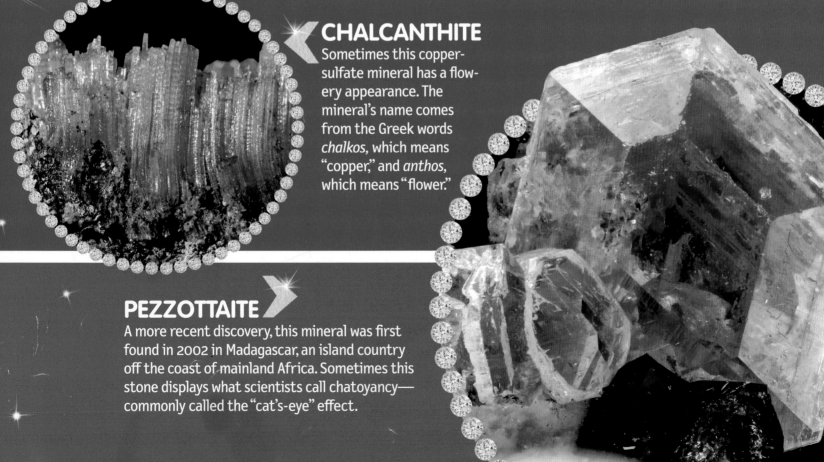

CHALCANTHITE

Sometimes this copper-sulfate mineral has a flow-ery appearance. The mineral's name comes from the Greek words *chalkos*, which means "copper," and *anthos*, which means "flower."

PEZZOTTAITE

A more recent discovery, this mineral was first found in 2002 in Madagascar, an island country off the coast of mainland Africa. Sometimes this stone displays what scientists call chatoyancy—commonly called the "cat's-eye" effect.

SINISTER STONES

Look but **don't touch!** You'd better leave these **creepy stones** alone—some say that those who didn't ended up paying the **ultimate price.**

Hope Diamond

HOPE DIAMOND

As the tale goes, a diamond was stolen from a temple in India in the mid-1600s, which angered the gods. They supposedly cursed the thief and future owners of the jewel. The diamond eventually wound up with France's King Louis XVI and his wife, Marie Antoinette—until they were beheaded in 1793. It later emerged in England, where the Hope family owned the blue jewel, until debt forced them to sell it. American socialite Evalyn Walsh McLean bought it next ... before several of her close family members met untimely deaths.

Now called the Hope Diamond, the 45.5-carat gem was donated to the Smithsonian Institution in 1958, but even that seemed cursed. The letter carrier who delivered it later had his leg crushed in a car accident. Although the lore might not be true, one eerie fact is: The blue diamond glows a bloody red when exposed to ultraviolet light. Now *that's* a colorful curse.

DELHI PURPLE SAPPHIRE

This supposedly cursed gem isn't a sapphire at all—it's actually an amethyst. According to its last owner, a British soldier stole the stone in the 1850s from a Hindu temple in India. A colonel brought the stone back to England, where his family went on to have troubles with health and money. In 1890 the stone was gifted to Edward Heron-Allen, a scientist and writer, who claimed to have bad luck after obtaining the jewel. He tried giving it away to several friends, but they all returned the stone, claiming the same bad luck had befallen them.

In an effort to ward off future woes, Heron-Allen locked the amethyst away inside seven boxes. He wrote a letter to

caution others of its powers, stating, "This stone is trebly accursed and is stained with blood, and the dishonour of everyone who has ever owned it."

The stone now resides in London's Natural History Museum, where it was donated in 1944 by Heron-Allen's daughter after his death. But the fake sapphire may be an imposter in more ways than one, as museum scientists suspect the curse may have been a hoax intended to stir up a good story.

STAR OF INDIA

The 563-carat blue star sapphire—the world's biggest gem-quality stone of its kind—is said to have been mined centuries ago in Sri Lanka under mysterious circumstances. But the stone led a pretty uneventful existence until 1964, when jewel thieves broke into the American Museum of Natural History in New York City and nabbed the sapphire.

The stone was among $410,000 worth of jewels ($3 million today) nabbed in the heist. The stars aligned to make the robbery possible—windows to the museum's gem hall had been left open, there was no security guard on duty in the room, and the batteries in the stone's display case alarm were dead. The stone was recovered soon after in a bus terminal locker in Miami, Florida, U.S.A.—but stories of the stone's curse linger on.

ORIGINALLY 112 CARATS, THE HOPE DIAMOND HAS BEEN CUT DOWN TO LESS THAN HALF ITS ORIGINAL SIZE.

Star of India

THE STAR OF INDIA'S THIEVES ALSO MADE OFF WITH A 100-CARAT RUBY AND A 116-CARAT BLACK SAPPHIRE.

Delhi Purple Sapphire

7 Flashy FACTS About ...
DAZZLING DIAMONDS

It's no wonder they say a diamond is forever: The revered rocks are the hardest natural substance on the planet. Here's the lowdown on these superstrong stones.

1 At 3,106 carats—about 1.4 pounds (0.6 kg)!—the **CULLINAN DIAMOND** is the **LARGEST ROUGH DIAMOND** ever discovered. It was cut into **106 DIFFERENT PIECES!**

2 Most **DIAMONDS FORM** dozens of miles **BELOW-GROUND,** where temperatures can reach up to **2370°F** (1300°C).

Aerial view of a diamond mine

3 Diamonds form in many **DIFFERENT COLORS,** depending on the **MINERALS PRESENT.**

4 In 1477 an **AUSTRIAN ARCHDUKE** became the first person to **PROPOSE MARRIAGE** with a **DIAMOND RING.**

5 People **BUY** more than **$72 BILLION** worth of diamonds **EACH YEAR.**

6 Volcanic eruptions **CARRY DIAMONDS** from **EARTH'S MANTLE** to the surface at more than **155 MILES AN HOUR** (249 km/h).

7 Romans believed **CUPID'S ARROW** had **DIAMOND TIPS.**

EXTRAV ANIMALS

Brilliant hues, dazzling dance moves, and bonkers bank accounts—these are some of the qualities boasted by the world's most splendorous species. From the mind-boggling colors that still baffle scientists to the eye-catching displays that have captured fascination for decades, the extravagance of these animals knows no bounds.

AGANT

These ANIMALS Aren't Actually BLUE!

MOOR FROG
The light blue coloring shows up for only a few days each year, when they visit ponds to breed.

MOST "BLUE" ANIMALS AREN'T REALLY BLUE.

HOW DO "BLUE" ANIMALS GET THEIR HUE?

Most blue animals get their color from structures that bounce light in such a way that our eyes perceive it as blue. Take the blue morpho butterfly: Its wings are covered in transparent scales, but it's the way that light bounces off those scales that makes them shimmer a metallic blue. Other animals, like the blue-footed booby, get their pigment from foods that they eat.

Of the world's more than 64,000 species of vertebrates (animals with backbones), only a couple can claim the title of "true blue." The mandarinfish and its cousin, the psychedelic mandarin, both have the rare ability to produce their own blue pigments. Many invertebrates (animals without backbones)—like sea stars—can make the color, too, but no one's quite sure why blue animals with backbones are so rare. One thing's for sure: It's not easy being blue.

Mandarinfish

BLUE-TONGUED SKINK
Their tongues may look blue, but the pigment in these appendages is actually brown.

BLUE-FOOTED BOOBY
The hue of this bird's famed feet comes from the fish it eats.

INDIAN PEACOCK
Structures within its feathers make this bird appear blue.

Blinged-Out
BUGS

Discover the **STUNNING SECRETS** behind some of nature's **MOST AMAZINGLY ADORNED** insects and spiders.

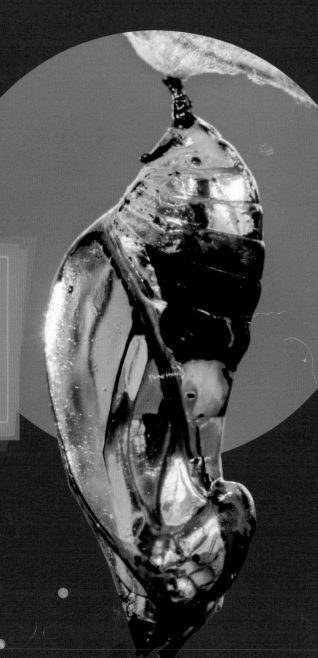

STRIKING GOLD

Soon-to-be butterflies wrap themselves in protective cases that come in an amazing array of colors. But the tigerwing butterfly might just have the most impressive of all. Wrapped inside gleaming gold chrysalises, tigerwing butterfly pupae decorate trees and branches inside cases that look like tiny holiday ornaments. How do these caterpillars create such a shimmering cocoon? The case's cells reflect light, making them look shiny.

MIRROR, MIRROR

With silver platelike spots on its body, the mirror spider could easily be confused for a tiny disco ball. The spots shrink when the spider is agitated, but when it's resting, the spots expand to cover its abdomen. Researchers think the mirrors could serve to camouflage this amazing arachnid by reflecting its natural surroundings. But if it were on a dance floor, this guy would be the center of attention.

COLOR BY NUMBER

Here's a bug that can color inside the lines: Beneath the wings of the Japanese jewel beetle are different numbers of chitin layers, the stuff that forms a bug's exoskeleton. The purple stripes are stacked with fewer layers than the green. As these chitin layers scramble light, they give off a beautiful multicolored sheen.

JEWEL BE SORRY!

The jewel caterpillar might look like candy, but eating this bug wouldn't be so sweet. Try taking a bite and the clear bubbles on the caterpillar's body will burst, buying it time to make a clean getaway while the diner's left with a mouthful of goo. Yuck!

FREAKY FIREWORKS

The explosive end of the planthopper nymph looks like something you'd see on the Fourth of July. And, in fact, these bugs' showy display isn't actually that different. Much like fireworks entertain, their waxy "tails" are meant to dazzle and distract predators that would otherwise try to eat them. The tail also may work to help planthoppers glide as they jump from leaf to leaf.

YELLOW TANG

Where: Pacific Ocean

Though almost an electric shade of yellow during the day, this fish literally changes overnight to a darker yellow as a means of avoiding detection. The only parts of this radiant fish that aren't so sunny are the white spines on either side of its tail, which will sting anyone that touches them.

SIDE-STRIPED PALM PIT VIPER

Where: Costa Rica and Panama

The color of this tropical tree-dwelling snake isn't much of a mystery—like lots of green animals, the viper's emerald hue keeps the reptile safely concealed among leafy plants.

COLORFUL

SILVERED LEAF MONKEY

Where: Southeast Asia

Though they're silver as adults, these monkeys are born a brilliant orange. Scientists have a few theories for why this might be the case: Some say the color makes it easier for moms to keep track of their youngsters as they start to explore the jungle. Others think the color might signal to the troop that there's a new monkey to babysit.

STUBBY SQUID >

Where: Northern Atlantic and Pacific Oceans

The internet went wild for this googly-eyed sea creature. According to the research team that captured the critter on camera, this little guy was likely searching for its next meal. Squid usually wear a "sticky mucus jacket" that attracts debris and makes the creatures less colorful—but they can quickly slip out of the disguise when prey comes by.

< SCARLET IBIS

Where: South America and the Caribbean

Like flamingos, these bright birds get their colorful plumage from carotenoids, the same pigments found in carrots. If they don't eat foods like shrimp and crabs, which contain these pigments, their color will fade. The brighter they are, the more attractive they are to a potential mate.

KINGDOM

In the animal world, bright colors bring attention and even communicate important messages.

< COBALT BLUE TARANTULA

Where: Myanmar and Thailand

This amazing arachnid gets its color from nanocrystals in its body. As for why the tarantula benefits from being blue, scientists are still trying to figure that out.

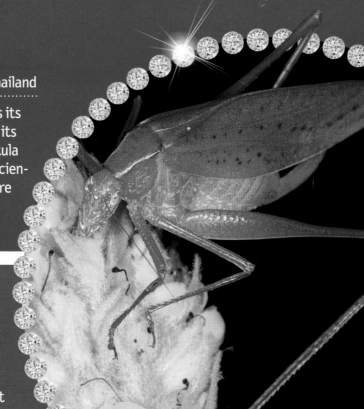

OBLONG-WINGED KATYDID >

Where: North America

Though usually green, these bugs have mutant genes that can cause them to be yellow, orange, or even neon pink.

THE RICHEST PETS OF ALL TIME

Meet nine animals with seriously lavish lifestyles.

Gourmet meals, diamond jewelry, designer clothes, and round-the-clock chauffeurs—just a day in the life of a superspoiled pet. Check out some of the richest fur balls (plus one chicken) to ever live.

BLACKIE
Where: Dorney, England

Think black cats are unlucky? Meet Blackie. Though his owner, English antiques dealer Ben Rea, owned 14 other felines, Blackie lived the longest and inherited his owner's fortune of approximately $12.5 million in 1988.

GUNTHER IV
Where: Miami, Florida, U.S.A.

Gunther IV is the top dog, holding the title of the richest pet ever. Countess Karlotta Liebenstein of Germany reportedly left her loyal pooch (and Gunther IV's dad) a $65 million fortune, which Gunther IV later inherited. In 2000 the canine was rumored to have spent some of his cash (through a lawyer) on a mansion in Miami Beach. Later the dog "bid" on the world's most expensive mushroom, but a restaurant owner won it for $35,000. No doubt Gunther could use the money for juicy steaks instead.

CONCHITA ▶▶▶▶
Where: Miami, Florida, U.S.A.

Chihua-wow! Often dressed in a pup-size wig, Conchita the Chihuahua wore four-legged fashions, strutted around nightclubs, and owned a $15,000 diamond necklace. When her owner, Miami socialite Gail Posner, passed away in 2010, Conchita's fancy treatment didn't end. She was left a $3 million trust fund.

TROUBLE ▶▶▶▶▶▶▶

Where: Sarasota, Florida, U.S.A.

Trouble's owner, businesswoman Leona Helmsley, insisted her pet be referred to as "Princess." And the Maltese lived up to her nickname! The pampered pooch traveled by stretch limousine to lunch dates, where she was hand-fed crab cakes. And when Helmsley died in 2007, she reportedly put aside roughly $12 million for Trouble—but practically nothing for her human family members.

TOBEY

Where: New York City

Born into money, Tobey the poodle was owned by Ella Wendel, a member of a rich New York City family in the early 20th century. Ella adored the pooch so much she had a miniature bed built in her own bedroom for Tobey to sleep in. Supposedly when the clan received multiple million-dollar offers for its mansion, the family refused. Why? Because Tobey needed a place to live.

GRUMPY CAT ▶▶▶▶

Where: Morristown, Arizona, U.S.A.

She may be famous for her frown, but Grumpy Cat is probably all smiles with a multimillion-dollar fortune. The internet star, whose real name is Tardar Sauce, has "written" several best-selling books, has a line of stuffed animals, and even stars in a movie. Her grumpy-looking face is actually caused by a natural underbite. So this cat's got plenty of reasons to smile.

GIGOO ▲

Where: Oxfordshire, England

This is one chicken that has something to strut about. Owned by British publisher Miles Blackwell and his wife, Gigoo was a Scots Dumpy hen—a rare breed with short legs. Though Gigoo's owners kept a number of other hens, Gigoo ultimately got the big bucks— about $9 million—when the owners passed away in 2001.

CHOUPETTE ▶▶▶▶▶

Where: Paris, France

She uses a $400 hair dryer, has two personal maids to comb her, and "writes" a blog read by tens of thousands of followers. Choupette is a silky Birman cat whose lifestyle any supermodel would envy. In 2014 she earned more than an estimated $3 million by modeling in ads. That's no surprise because her owner is famous clothing designer Karl Lagerfeld.

TOMMASO

Where: Rome, Italy

Here's a rags-to-riches tale: Italian street cat Tommaso hopped into the lap of luxury when an elderly woman named Maria Assunta adopted him. Though going from alley cat to pampered pet probably improved his diet, Tommaso became a real fat cat in 2011 after his owner reportedly left him a cushy $13 million.

Gold-veined skin protects
the red-eyed tree frog's eyes
when it SLEEPS.

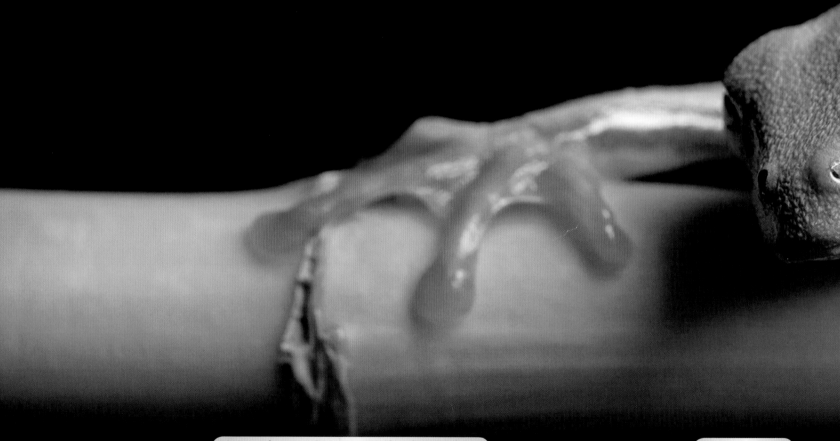

Northern Spiny-Tailed Gecko

Cuttlefish

MORE AMAZING ► EYES

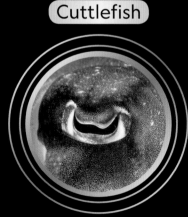

Macaw

WHAT'S WITH THE CREEPY PEEPERS?

Called nictitating membranes, these lustrous layers of translucent tissue act as an extra set of eyelids. They protect the frog's eyes as it snoozes during the day, just like a human's eyelids do. But the special eye shields also let some of the frog's radiant red eyes shine through, making predators think the animal is still awake and on alert. Even though it's sleeping, enough light shines through the membranes for the frog to detect nearby threats.

Dogs, cats, camels, and even polar bears have these extra eyelids. Camels benefit from having them in dry, hot deserts where sand constantly blows through the air. But no other animal's eyelids are even close to being as glitzy as these.

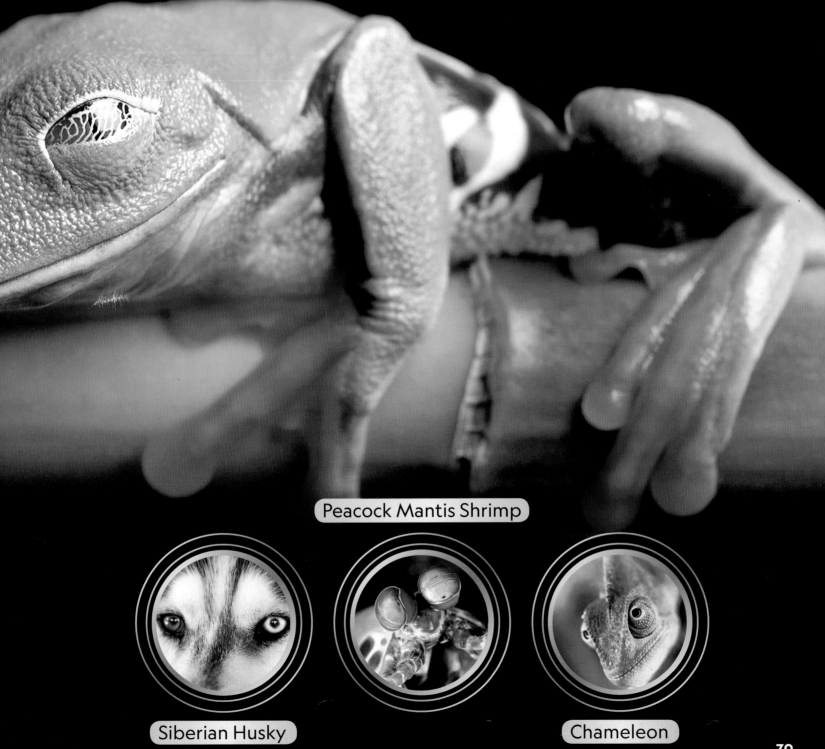

Peacock Mantis Shrimp

Siberian Husky

Chameleon

Brilliant BIRDS

Check out some of the flashiest **FEATHERS, DANCES,** and **OTHER AWESOME ANTICS** from the avian world.

DOUBLE TROUBLE
Scientists used to think a bird could either have an elaborate song or flashy feathers—but developing the two together would take too much energy. Male tanagers outdo their bird relatives with the showstopping ability to impress females with both.

ROYAL TREATMENT
Victoria crowned pigeons, the largest of the world's pigeons, have elegant blue crests that look like delicate lace. A male tries to win over a female by bowing before her, wagging his tail, and letting out a loud, hollow call. Now, if only he could open the door!

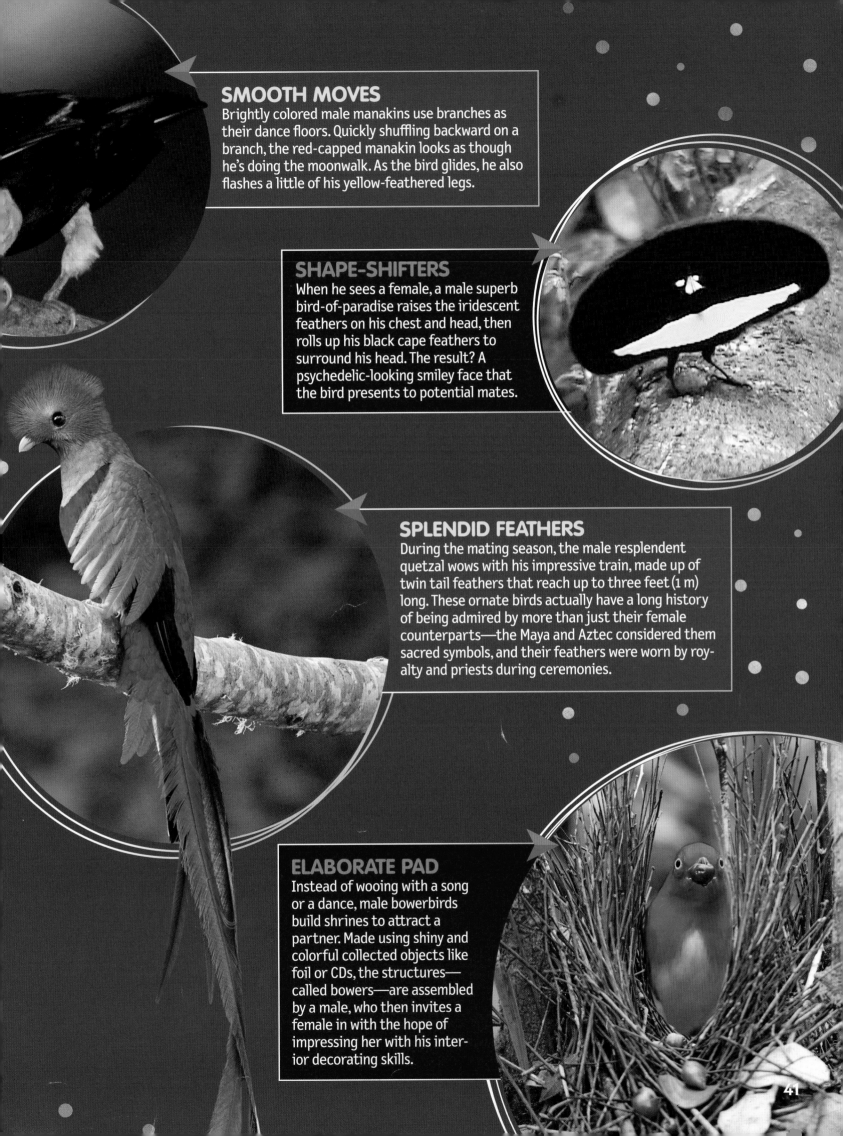

SMOOTH MOVES

Brightly colored male manakins use branches as their dance floors. Quickly shuffling backward on a branch, the red-capped manakin looks as though he's doing the moonwalk. As the bird glides, he also flashes a little of his yellow-feathered legs.

SHAPE-SHIFTERS

When he sees a female, a male superb bird-of-paradise raises the iridescent feathers on his chest and head, then rolls up his black cape feathers to surround his head. The result? A psychedelic-looking smiley face that the bird presents to potential mates.

SPLENDID FEATHERS

During the mating season, the male resplendent quetzal wows with his impressive train, made up of twin tail feathers that reach up to three feet (1 m) long. These ornate birds actually have a long history of being admired by more than just their female counterparts—the Maya and Aztec considered them sacred symbols, and their feathers were worn by royalty and priests during ceremonies.

ELABORATE PAD

Instead of wooing with a song or a dance, male bowerbirds build shrines to attract a partner. Made using shiny and colorful collected objects like foil or CDs, the structures—called bowers—are assembled by a male, who then invites a female in with the hope of impressing her with his interior decorating skills.

COOL CRABS

Three cheers for these peppy creatures!

These small but mighty pom-pom crabs are tiny indeed—usually growing only an inch (2.5 cm) wide. Living in shallow tropical waters, these crabs show off their brilliant bling—anemones they collect and carry—as they dance across the ocean floor.

- **RANGE:** Indian and Pacific Oceans
- **HABITAT:** Seabeds and coral reefs
- **DIET:** An omnivore that eats both meat and plants

Pom-pom crabs walk along the seafloor on striped legs.

The anemones' tentacles are armed with stinging cells to ward off would-be attackers.

The anemones help the crabs catch food and provide protection from predators. They can even pick up debris from the crab's home.

Pom-pom crabs carry anemones in each claw.

Females carry their eggs on their abdomen for roughly two weeks, until they are ready to hatch.

More ANIMAL ACCESSORIES

OCTOPUSES
Build shelters out of coconut shells, glass jars, and other discarded containers

ORB-WEAVING SPIDER
Decorates its web with whatever junk it can find

ANCIENT INSECTS
Had feathery tubes that held on to debris

ASSASSIN BUG
Wears the bodies of dead ants

7 Flashy FACTS About ...
GLAMOROUS GOODS

You've probably heard about caviar and cashmere—but animals create a wealth of other rare and pricey products.

1 Smoked cheese called **PULE,** made from the milk of just **200 DONKEYS** in Siberia, can sell for more than **$1,000** a kilogram.

2 In silk production—an **ANCIENT PRACTICE** originating in China— it takes the threads of a **THOUSAND COCOONS** to create a single silk shirt.

3 Hair combed from South American **VICUÑAS,** members of the camel family, is used to make one of the world's most **LUXURIOUS** and **COSTLY FIBERS.**

4 A foot-long (0.3-m) egg laid by a now extinct **ELEPHANT BIRD** sold at auction for more than **$100,000.**

5 One of the world's **MOST EXPENSIVE COFFEES** is brewed from beans picked out of **ELEPHANT POOP.**

BLACK IVORY COFFEE®
Net weight: 35 grams

6 For the price of a **SMALL CAR,** you can buy a **BOTTLE OF HONEY** that's been extracted from deep inside **MINERAL-RICH** Turkish caves.

7 Only one of roughly every **10,000 WILD OYSTERS** will contain a **NATURAL PEARL** of value.

45

SCALE TALES

Tropical piranha

A fish's **spectacular scales** aren't just for show. Scales are useful in lots of ways—they help a fish blend in with its surroundings, ward off **predators,** and even **allow scientists** to better understand the human body.

Rainbow darter

VICIOUS FISH?

By now you've surely heard the terrifying tale of the piranha. The bloodthirsty fish, equipped with razor-sharp teeth, prowls the water eager to eat the flesh off any animal that crosses its path. Or, at least that's the popular belief.

The truth? The sparkly Amazonian swimmers aren't as vicious as you might think. Sure, they've been known to pack a dangerous bite—but the piranhas' scales tell us they'd rather swim under the radar than cause fear. Although the scales might look showy to us, they actually make the fish harder to spot from overhead. As birds and other predators along the riverbank search for a meal, the piranha's sparkly scales match the sunlight seen reflecting off the water's surface, allowing the glitzy fish to go undetected.

FLASH MOB

Some fish are good at blending in, whereas others find a way to stand out. On its own, a blue jack mackerel doesn't stand a chance of surviving a predator's ambush. At only 10 inches (25 cm) long, it's an easy snack for a hungry dolphin or shark. So these small metallic fish employ a flashy tactic.

Banding together with thousands of their closest friends, mackerels form a giant shimmering ball. Swirling around in a glistening swarm, the fish try to pass for one colossal, shiny mega-creature. This optical illusion is designed to create confusion and scare off would-be predators hoping to eat them.

Scientists are studying swarms like this to learn more about the human body, from how our brains work to how cancer spreads. Their findings might even offer up information that could one day be used to navigate self-driving cars.

READING RAINBOWS

Ever wonder what happens to your skin when you get a cut? It turns out scientists also looked to fish to answer this question. In 2016 researchers at Duke University, in North Carolina, U.S.A., conducted a study to examine the scales of zebrafish—but not just any zebrafish. To see how the fish healed in real time, the researchers bred their fish to have Technicolor scales. Each cell on a scale could shine in thousands of different color combos, giving it a unique "skinbow." By tracking the cells with their unique color codes, the team could see how cells grew and moved to cover a wound.

Doctors in Brazil have taken the healing power of scales one step further—by outfitting their patients with fish skin. After supply shortages left burn victims with a need for bandages, doctors turned to tilapia to dress the wounds. The fish's skin can stay on a lot longer than a regular bandage before needing to be changed, and even has painkilling powers.

Scientists have already learned a lot from studying fish—what story will their scales reveal next?

FISH SCALES ARE COMMONLY USED TO MAKE LIPSTICK.

A doctor uses fish scales to treat a patient.

Blue jack mackerel

ANCIENT FISH SCALES WERE COATED IN THE SAME ENAMEL THAT COVERS YOUR TEETH.

POSH
PAST

Buried loot recovered after centuries undisturbed. Posh palaces fit for kings. History has given us a treasure trove of ancient artifacts, royal relics, and stories of striking it rich. And the bling left behind reveals amazing secrets about the lavish lifestyles of people from earlier times.

49

Ancient Romans used SNAILS to dye their clothes purple.

MORE NATURAL DYES

RED
Cochineal Insects

YELLOW
Rhubarb Roots

WHY USE SLIMY CREATURES TO CREATE GLAMOROUS GARB?

Purple used to be a hard color to come by. In ancient times, the only way to produce it was with tiny snails found exclusively in the Tyre region of the Mediterranean Sea. Being rare and time-consuming to create meant the dye was expensive. It took more than 9,000 of these mollusks to make a single gram of dye. The snails were boiled for days, giving off a foul odor. Then their chemical compounds were harvested and exposed to heat and light to make the coveted color.

   Because it was so pricey, purple soon became an exclusive symbol of royalty and wealth in Rome. Purple's royal popularity spread, reaching countries like Egypt and Persia (now called Iran). Queen Elizabeth I of England even forbade anyone outside the royal family from wearing the color. Talk about the power of purple!

Snails were boiled in lead containers to make purple dye.

BLUE
Cuttlefish Ink

ORANGE
Onion Skins

GREEN
Eucalyptus

PINK
Avocado Pits

Legends of GOLD

Learn the truth behind these FANTASTICALLY FICTIONAL TALES of WEALTH.

BURIED BOOTY

Treasured myth: Leprechauns guard pots of gold at the ends of rainbows.

Pure facts: No one's quite sure where this legend originated. Some say Vikings once buried treasure in Ireland and left it behind, where the mythical leprechauns later found it. They reburied the loot in their own spots, and rainbows formed overhead, pointing to the gold. In reality, rainbows don't have an end point—they're circles. The multicolored arcs form when sunlight hits raindrops. The droplets act like prisms, bending the light at different angles to create a rainbow effect. The circular pattern is thanks to the circle of the sun.

MAGIC TOUCH

Treasured myth: King Midas turned everything he touched to gold.

Pure facts: As the Greek myth goes, a fairy granted King Midas—not satisfied with his wealth—his wish that all he touched turned to gold. The king was finally pleased—until his food, water, and even his own daughter turned to solid gold. Of course, people don't really have this power. But the story is a reminder of the danger of getting too greedy.

CITY OF RICHES

Treasured myth: Hidden somewhere in the world is an immense treasure trove of riches called El Dorado.

Pure facts: The legend started with 16th-century Spanish explorers in South America who supposedly heard stories about a tribe in the Andes Mountains. When a new chieftain rose to power, he would be covered with gold dust, and gold and precious jewels would be tossed into the nearby lake to appease an underwater god. The explorers called the chief El Dorado, Spanish for "the gilded one." To this day rumors still swirl about a city of secret loot.

SPINNING A STORY

Treasured myth: A strange creature can spin straw into gold.

Pure facts: In the German fairy tale "Rumpelstiltskin," the mischievous character spins shimmering threads in exchange for gifts and favors. Of course, the tale is just a made-up story. But in the real world, one type of bacteria does have the ability to turn liquid gold to solid nuggets—part of a defense mechanism that helps the bacteria avoid toxins in the liquid. Now that rocks.

SWANKY STONE

Treasured myth: A "philosopher's stone" can turn lead into gold.

Pure facts: Alchemy is the ancient practice of trying to convert other metals into gold. We know now that lead and gold are two different chemical elements. But it turns out modern scientists have found a way to really make the shape-shifting happen—with a fancy machine called a particle accelerator. Just one problem: The process costs more than the gold is actually worth.

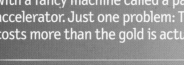

CORONATION EGG
This decorative yellow egg was an Easter gift from Tsar Nicholas II of Russia to his wife. One of many extravagant egg creations from famed jeweler Fabergé, this one features diamonds and a plush velvet lining.

BRONZE HEAD
Archaeologists were stumped by the seemingly advanced craftsmanship of the bronze relics—including this green-and-gold statue—belonging to China's kingdom of Shu. The relics were recovered from the Chinese village of Sanxingdui, which was mysteriously abandoned around 1000 B.C.

ROYAL RI

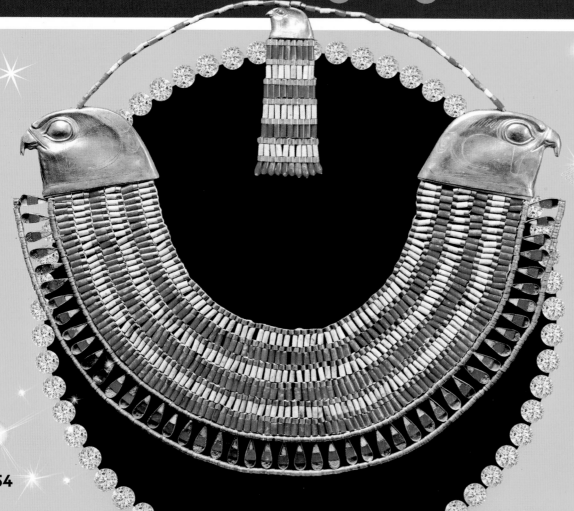

CARNELIAN NECKLACE
Found in the tomb of Egyptian princess Neferuptah, this orange-and-white falcon necklace was thought to have powers that warded off evil in the afterlife.

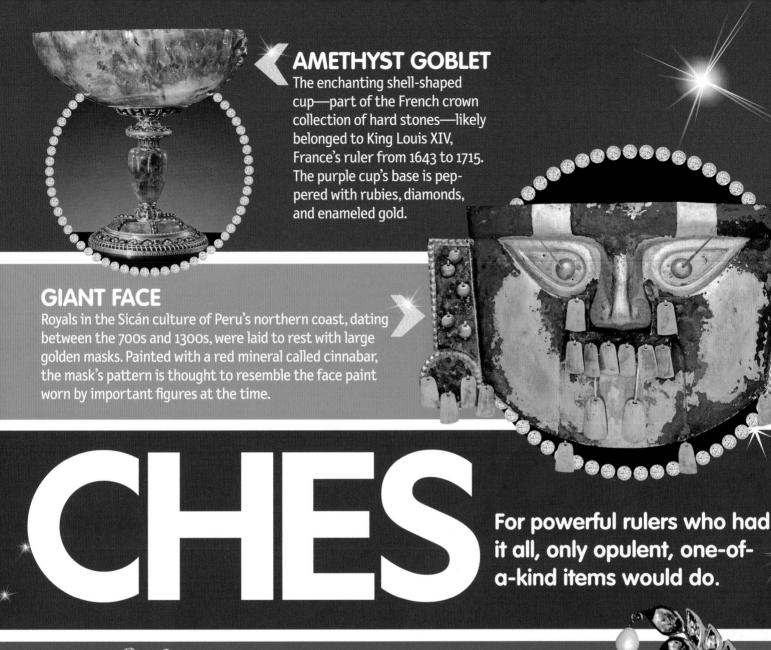

AMETHYST GOBLET
The enchanting shell-shaped cup—part of the French crown collection of hard stones—likely belonged to King Louis XIV, France's ruler from 1643 to 1715. The purple cup's base is peppered with rubies, diamonds, and enameled gold.

GIANT FACE
Royals in the Sicán culture of Peru's northern coast, dating between the 700s and 1300s, were laid to rest with large golden masks. Painted with a red mineral called cinnabar, the mask's pattern is thought to resemble the face paint worn by important figures at the time.

CHES

For powerful rulers who had it all, only opulent, one-of-a-kind items would do.

LAPIS LAZULI PENDANT
The king of Ur, an ancient city in Iraq, had this splendid pendant custom-made for the king of Mari, a Syrian city connected to Ur by the Euphrates River. The lion head is thought to represent the king of all animals, the blue bird body to represent a connection to heaven and Earth, and the fish tail to represent a connection between the two waterside kingdoms.

TURBAN ORNAMENT
Cloth headdresses called turbans were worn by men all across Asia's Mogul Empire, whose rulers constructed India's Taj Mahal. But decorative plumes were a status symbol reserved only for royalty. This flourishing pink example is covered in rubies, emeralds, and jade.

LOST AND FOUND
TREASURES

For centuries, **treasures worth billions** of dollars have been lost or hidden around the world. Professional treasure hunters travel the globe in **search of the riches,** but others are lucky enough to accidentally stumble upon the loot. No matter how they're discovered, these age-old valuables tell us important things about the past. Check out three stories of **lost treasures found.**

Coins recovered from a 16th century Spanish galleon

SUNKEN GOLD

In the summer of 2013, Rick Schmitt and his family dove into the waters off eastern Florida, U.S.A. For years the treasure hunters had been searching for riches in the area, famous for its old shipwrecks. Gliding over tangled seaweed on the Atlantic Ocean floor, they suddenly saw something glittering in their flashlight beams—$300,000 worth of gold chains, coins, and jewelry. The riches date back to the 1700s, when Spanish ships sailed back and forth between Spain and Florida, then a Spanish colony. The ships, called galleons, often ferried treasure from North and South America to Europe. In July 1715, a hurricane sank 11 galleons near Florida's coast, scattering valuables along the seafloor. Nearly 300 years later, the Schmitts found only a portion of this loot, part of which was given to a museum. But more riches from the wrecked galleons linger somewhere at the bottom of the ocean.

PALACE PRIZE

In the bustling city center of Kathmandu, Nepal, in Asia, sits a sprawling palace complex known as Hanuman Dhoka. Dating from at least the 16th century, the palace housed Nepal's royal family until 1886. Even after the family moved, it was used for important ceremonies. Later the complex became a museum. In 2011 workers began renovating the former residence. Hidden under the terrace of the king's living room, they discovered three safes and a tank filled with gold jewelry, bows with silver arrows, and gold masks. Thought to be at least 500-year-old offerings made to Hindu gods and goddesses worshipped by the Nepali people, the treasure trove weighed more than 450 pounds (204 kg)—about the same as two refrigerators. No one knows for sure why the loot, worth hundreds of thousands of dollars, was placed here. But with the treasure on exhibit, the renovated palace museum won't just be spruced up—it'll be blinged out!

MAYA RICHES

During a 2012 expedition to the jungles of northern Guatemala, a team of archaeologists crouched beneath a canopy of giant leaves to excavate an ancient Maya temple. As the team dug around the site, they made an exciting find: a tomb filled with precious stones and ancient bones. Maya hieroglyphics on a jar in the burial chamber revealed that the bones may have belonged to a warrior queen named Lady K'abel. Jade jewels—the gems most prized by the Maya—surrounded the queen's remains. A ceramic plate resembling a battle shield also lay in the crypt. The bones and other objects were from the seventh century, the height of the Maya Empire that once stretched across Central America and southern Mexico. The exact worth of the treasure hasn't been calculated—but most people agree this find is priceless.

A limestone monument of Lady K'abel

Hanuman Dhoka

7 Flashy FACTS About ...

A-LIST ACCESSORIES

These highly prized items belonged to some of history's most famous figures.

1 THE DUCHESS OF WINDSOR once owned a bejeweled FLAMINGO BROOCH designed by LUXURY JEWELER CARTIER.

2 AN ASTRONAUT traveled into SPACE with a WATCH used by aviator AMELIA EARHART on her transatlantic flights.

3 A collector dropped more than $10,000 for the KEYS to THOMAS EDISON'S "INVENTION FACTORY."

4

The **PINAFORE**
worn by actress Julie Andrews
in ***THE SOUND
OF MUSIC*** sold for
$1.56 MILLION
at auction.

5

Musician Wolfgang Amadeus
MOZART sported custom-made
SHOE BUCKLES fashioned
from **SILVER AND BRASS.**

6

One of Leonardo da Vinci's
PAINTINGS
sold for **$450 MILLION.**

On her wedding day, former first lady
JACQUELINE KENNEDY
wore a bracelet with
25 DIAMONDS and **18 PEARLS—**
a gift from **PRESIDENT KENNEDY.**

7

Astounding ARTIFACTS

Discover the **STORIES** behind some of the world's most **INCREDIBLE ANCIENT FINDS.**

VIP VESSELS

Unearthed by accident in Bulgaria in 1949, the Panagyurishte treasure is still a bit of a mystery. Experts think the nine gold objects, totaling 13 pounds (6 kg), were probably created around the fourth century B.C. for wealthy rulers to use in rituals. What surprised archaeologists about the find was the unique style of the goods. One large vessel features scenes from Greek mythology. Others are delicately crafted to look like animal heads, including a deer and a goat.

AFGHAN TREASURES

In 1978 an archaeologist in northern Afghanistan made a massive find when he uncovered six tombs filled with golden riches. The site was once part of Bactria, a region that fell along an ancient network of trade routes called the Silk Road. When the excavation was done, the golden objects totaled more than 20,000, representing cultures from all around the world. Among the glittering goods were Chinese dragons, Greek rings, and Roman and Indian coins—but one of the most dazzling finds was an intricate golden crown found buried with one of the dead.

VIKING LOOT

Dubbed the Galloway Hoard, the 1,000-year-old lot of Viking loot is one of Britain's biggest treasure finds. After a man in Scotland reported the find, an archaeologist was called in to help unearth and identify the artifacts. Buried beneath the field was a wealth of gold and silver jewelry, some carefully packaged inside a metal vessel. Historians think this vessel may have been stolen from a medieval Scottish monastery. Talk about stirring up ancient history!

HUGE HAUL

For 1,300 years a grand stash of buried treasure went undisturbed in the English countryside. Then in 2009, a man with a metal detector discovered the loot, soon named the Staffordshire Hoard. More than 3,500 items were recovered, mostly made of gold and silver. Among the items were sword fittings and other military items, leading experts to think the bling belonged to a group of warriors.

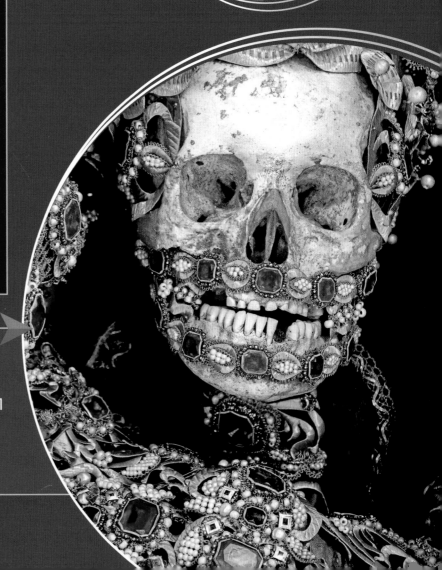

BEJEWELED SKELETONS

Adorned with sparkling gems, golden jewelry, and fine clothes, these skeletons are drop-dead gorgeous. The decorated bones went largely unseen and unknown until 2008, when an art historian started digging into the story behind the skeletons. Called "catacomb saints," the bejeweled bodies were tucked away in European churches to protect people and represent the afterlife.

Golden MASK

For more than 3,000 years, this famous Egyptian treasure sat buried below a desert in a tomb of riches. Thought to belong to King Tutankhamun—the boy who became Egypt's ruler at just nine years old—the intricately crafted mask is now one of history's most iconic artifacts.

YEAR CREATED: Circa 1323 B.C.

HEIGHT: 21 inches (54 cm)

DISCOVERED IN: Luxor, Egypt

SCALED AT 150%

The snake figure on the mask's forehead represents Wadjet, the cobra goddess of Lower Egypt, while a bird figure represents Nekhbet, the vulture goddess of Upper Egypt. Together the two figures symbolize power and protection.

The eyes of the mask are made from quartz and obsidian, a rock formed from lava.

So his spirit would recognize his body in the afterlife, King Tut's mask—designed to look just like his real face—rested on the pharaoh's head inside his tomb.

Egyptian royals wore makeup to give their eyes an almond shape. This mask's eyes are outlined in a blue stone called lapis lazuli.

Pharaohs like King Tut often wore false beards—like the narrow, braided beard on his mask—for special occasions.

Archaeologists unearthed the golden mask in 1922. Covered with stones and glass, the entire mask weighs 22 pounds (10 km).

INCREDIBLE PALACES

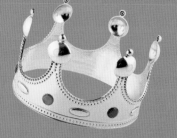

For centuries rulers have been living like, well, kings. Discover some of the most opulent royal residences on the planet.

PALACE OF VERSAILLES
Where: France

Built to impress, this posh palace is the former home of French royalty. Perhaps its most notable resident, King Louis XIV helped elevate the palace to five-star status. Each morning the king reportedly greeted his entourage as he left his bedroom and walked down the 220-foot (67-m)-long Hall of Mirrors, lined with 357 reflective panels. Outside, the grounds' mile-long (1.6-km) Grand Canal hosted King Louis XIV's fleet of vessels, including two gondolas he received as gifts.

ALHAMBRA ▶▶▶▶
Where: Spain

Posted high at the top of a hill, this Spanish palace was strategically placed for members of the former Nasrid dynasty to look out on the city below. Gardens and courtyards are sprinkled throughout the grounds, and intricate stucco carvings decorate the palace walls. Once painted a variety of vibrant colors, only traces of paint remain today.

ISTANA NURUL IMAN

Where: Brunei

Home to the sultan of Brunei, the world's largest royal residence spans a whopping 2,152,783 square feet (200,000 sq m). The gigantic palace features 1,788 rooms—including 257 bathrooms! Lavish luxuries are everywhere: The palace possesses 564 chandeliers, a 110-car garage, five swimming pools, and a temperature-controlled stable for 200 ponies.

BUCKINGHAM PALACE >>>

Where: England

A team of 21 chefs preps special dinners hosted at this royal British residence, featuring dishes served on golden platters, like lobster-stuffed filet of sole. A gold-covered horse-drawn coach, used in every coronation, sits in waiting for the reigning monarch. The regal pad, with 775 rooms, also boasts a post office, police station, doctor's office, movie theater, and pool.

NEUSCHWANSTEIN CASTLE >>>>>>

Where: Germany

Stepping into this Bavarian hilltop castle is like stepping into a fairy tale. Built for King Ludwig II, also fittingly known as the "Fairy Tale King," Neuschwanstein was designed to be a regal retreat. Does this castle look familiar? The picture-perfect building is rumored to be the real-life inspiration for Disneyland's Sleeping Beauty Castle.

◄◄ WINTER PALACE
Where: Russia

There's no shortage of gold in this glitzy residence, once home to former Russian monarchs. Reconstructed after a fire in 1837, the Gold Drawing Room shines with walls and vaulted ceilings gilded in gold. Another decked-out spot, the Armorial Hall, is lined with gold columns and guarded on either side by grand sculptures of Russian warriors. Even the Grand Church inside the palace is blinged out with gold-leafed paint.

◄◄ FORBIDDEN CITY
Where: China

Up until 1912, the Forbidden City was the Chinese imperial palace. And humans weren't the only ones living large in the posh pad— dogs in the palace got the royal treatment, too. The canines of royal residents lived in pavilions with marble floors, slept on silk cushions, and had their every need tended to by special servants.

PENA PALACE ▶▶▶▶▶
Where: Portugal

The showstopping colors of this strangely assembled pad seem to jump out of the lush forest that surrounds it. The mishmash of looks outside is matched by a hodgepodge of styles inside, with some rooms reflecting Middle Eastern culture and others giving a more baroque European feel.

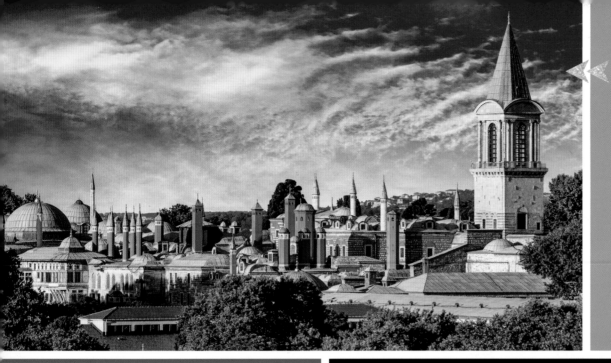

TOPKAPI PALACE
Where: Turkey

Overlooking the Bosporus, this top-notch spot served as the home of sultans in the Ottoman Empire for 400 years. Every time a new sultan moved in, the newcomer would add another section to the palace to match his taste. The result? A gigantic, mystifying maze of buildings within the palace complex.

MYSORE PALACE >>>>>
Where: India

At night, the outside of this former home of Mysore rulers is illuminated with 97,000 lights. Floors inside the palace shine, too, thanks to inlaid semiprecious stones. During the annual Dasara festival—a Mysore tradition—a jewel-encrusted golden throne emerges from the palace strong room for viewing, and a parade hits the streets. The golden howdah, or elephant seat, is the star of the show. The 1,650-pound (748-kg) seat is carried through the city by a very carefully selected elephant that goes through years of training before getting the coveted gig.

SCHÖNBRUNN PALACE
Where: Austria

This palace has plenty of claims to fame. In 1752 it became the site of the world's first zoo, and 10 years later—at the age of just six years old—legendary musician Wolfgang Amadeus Mozart performed a concert here for royal residents. A few years later Mozart came back to perform in the palace's orangery, which, at 610 feet (186 m) long, is the world's longest stretch of the citrus-growing trees.

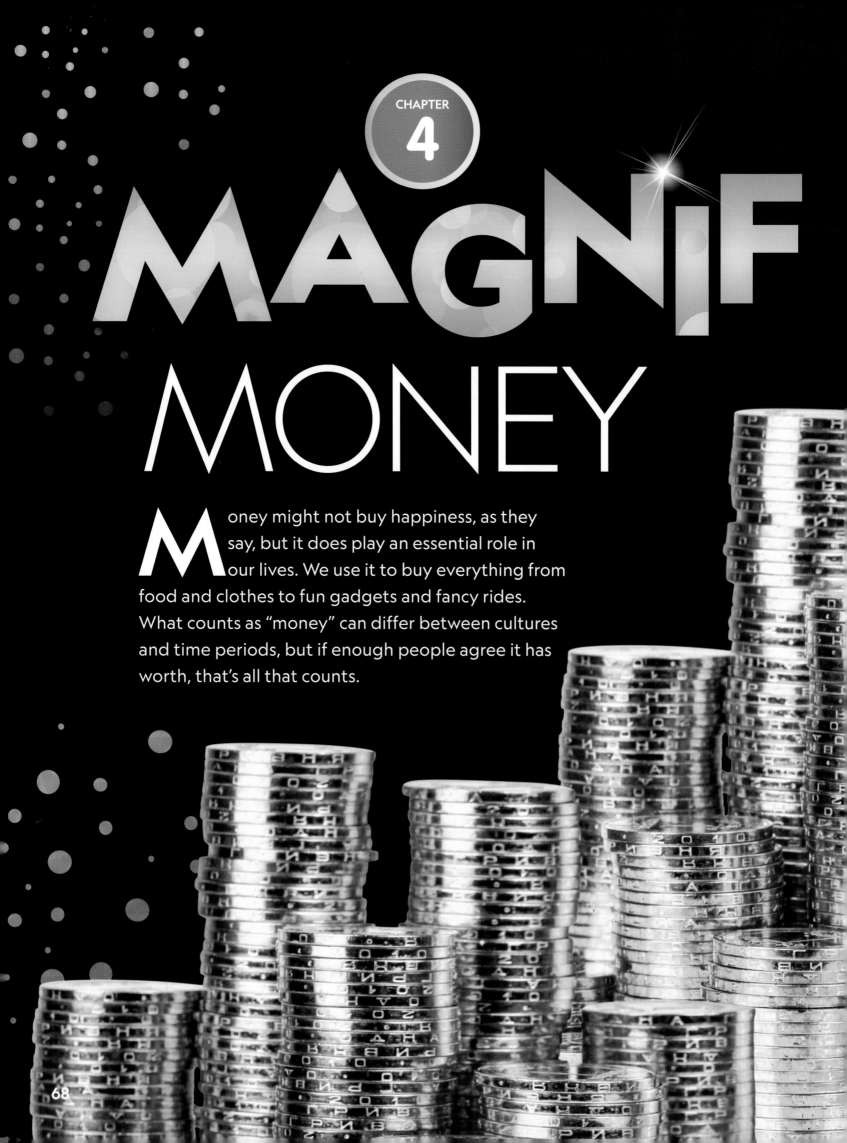

MAGNIF
MONEY

Money might not buy happiness, as they say, but it does play an essential role in our lives. We use it to buy everything from food and clothes to fun gadgets and fancy rides. What counts as "money" can differ between cultures and time periods, but if enough people agree it has worth, that's all that counts.

ICENT

Rich
TRADITIONS

We've all heard about **LUCKY PENNIES** and **FOUR-LEAF CLOVERS**. But cultures across the world have their own **BELIEFS** when it comes to striking it **RICH**.

CHARMING ART
Japan

The art of origami—folding paper into decorative shapes—has been a Japanese tradition for centuries. To the Japanese, origami frogs can bring good luck. The belief is tied to the Japanese language. *Kaeru,* the Japanese word for frog, is a homonym for the Japanese word meaning "to return." So, by putting an origami frog in one's wallet, it's thought that money will return to the person carrying it.

Others in Japan, particularly business owners, use waving cat figurines as lucky charms. The *maneki-neko* cat is widely used in Japanese stores and restaurants. The figurine originated from a Japanese legend in which a cat saved a priest from being struck by lightning.

LUCKY UNDIES
China

As Chinese legend goes, there was a beast called Nian that had the body of a bull and the head of a lion. The monstrous creature wreaked havoc on villagers—until they discovered it was afraid of the color red.

Today it's tradition for celebrants of the Chinese New Year to wear red underwear, which is supposed to bring wealth and prosperity in the year ahead. The traditional belief is that your *ben ming nian*—the year of your Chinese zodiac, which comes around once every 12 years—will be filled with bad luck, but donning the lucky color can help fend off evil forces.

BIRD'S-EYE VIEW
South Africa

Vultures have a reputation as ugly, scary scavengers, but these rare birds actually play an important role in their ecosystem—consuming the dead animals they find thanks to their excellent eyesight.

In South African folklore, vultures are said to have such good vision that they can see into the future. Poachers have taken advantage of the belief to turn a profit and sell the animals as good luck charms. But conservationists are working hard to stop poachers from harming these helpful fliers.

SPIDEY CENTS
Trinidad and Tobago

Most people cringe when they find a spider in their house. Some might even scream and squirm thanks to arachnophobia, the fear of spiders. But in the Caribbean country of Trinidad and Tobago, spiders are welcome visitors.

A brown "money spider" is a symbol of good luck, especially if it crawls on you! If you put the creepy-crawly in your pocket, you'll be even better off—that pocket will never be empty again. Brown grasshoppers are good signs, too, but beware of green ones. Those mean bad news for your bank account.

50,000 SHILLING
Where: Uganda

Mountain gorillas—like the one on this yellow bill—are among the most elusive creatures in the central African jungle. But that doesn't mean they're small: Mature males, called silverbacks, can weigh up to 485 pounds (220 kg). The apes aren't just elusive—they're also critically endangered. Fewer than a thousand exist in the wild.

100 FLORIN ➤
Where: Aruba

How'd the Colombian four-eyed frog, seen on this green bill, earn its name? In addition to the two eyes on its head, the amphibian has a pretend pair above its back legs. Likely designed to ward off predators, these fake peepers pack a dangerous punch—the "eyes" are really glands packed with poison.

WILD BILLS

5 DOLLAR
Where: New Zealand

The yellow-eyed penguin on this orange bill—known to the local Maori people as the *hoiho*—is one of the rarest penguins on the planet. People wanting to catch a peek at the high-profile penguins, found only in New Zealand, contribute some $70 million a year to the country's economy.

50 RUBLE

Where: Belarus

On money they may be purple, but in the wild these bears are all-brown. Carnivorous brown bears live in parts of North America, Europe, and Asia. Their enormous home ranges can extend up to a thousand square miles (2,590 sq km).

50 RAND

Where: South Africa

The most social of all cats, lions live in groups called prides. Males defend the pride's territory while females go off to hunt for the group. The color of a male's mane gives a clue to how old he is—the darker the mane, the older the cat. The color of the bill, on the other hand, gives a clue to how much the bill is worth.

Some nations put people's portraits on their money— but these banknotes feature colorful creatures instead.

1,000 RUFIYAA

Where: Maldives

The green sea turtle on this blue bill gets its name from the color of its fat. Unlike most other sea turtles, an adult green sea turtle eats mostly plants. Scientists think the green foods give the turtle's fat its green color.

10 REAIS

Where: Brazil

Though they don't look it from this pink bill, macaws are some of the most vibrantly colored birds in the world. They're also some of the most intelligent—some have even been taught to understand and speak words.

7 Flashy FACTS About ...

SPLENDID
SPENDING

You won't believe the price tags on these purchases.

1 George Washington once spent **$5,000** in today's money on **ICE CREAM** in just one summer.

2 A rare **MISPRINTED STAMP** of an upside-down airplane sold at an auction for more than **$1.1 MILLION.**

3 On average, Americans spend **$2.7 BILLION** on **HALLOWEEN CANDY** each year.

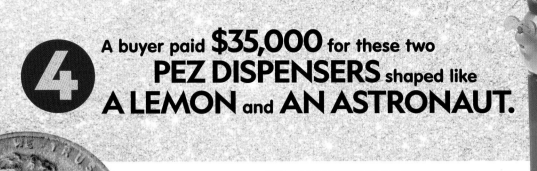

4 A buyer paid **$35,000** for these two **PEZ DISPENSERS** shaped like **A LEMON** and **AN ASTRONAUT.**

5 During World War II, the **U.S. MINT** accidentally made **BRONZE PENNIES** that are now worth more than **$1 MILLION** each.

6 One tech company created a **$5 MILLION SOLID-GOLD TOILET.**

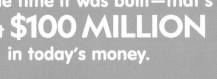

7 The White House cost **$232,000** at the time it was built—that's about **$100 MILLION** in today's money.

Swanky SPACE STATION

Costing more than $100 billion to create, the International Space Station (ISS) holds the record as the most expensive human-made object. Take a look at some of the fantastic features that make this superior research center a total blast.

- **SPEED:** 17,500 miles an hour (28,164 km/h)
- **ORBIT AROUND EARTH:** Every 90 minutes
- **TOURIST DOLLARS DROPPED:** $40 million

ASTRONAUTS ON BOARD THE ISS SEE 16 SUNRISES AND SUNSETS A DAY.

SOLAR PANELS ON THE SPACE STATION PRODUCE ENOUGH ELECTRICITY TO POWER MORE THAN 40 HOMES.

Since the facility opened, hundreds of scientific experiments have been conducted in its laboratories. Astronauts have tested everything from what happens when you wring out a wet towel in space to how jellyfish adapt to living outside of Earth.

To stay healthy, astronauts spend up to two hours a day exercising with special space equipment. Instead of a seat, the stationary bike has handles for gripping. A treadmill has a harness that astronauts wear so they don't drift off during their run.

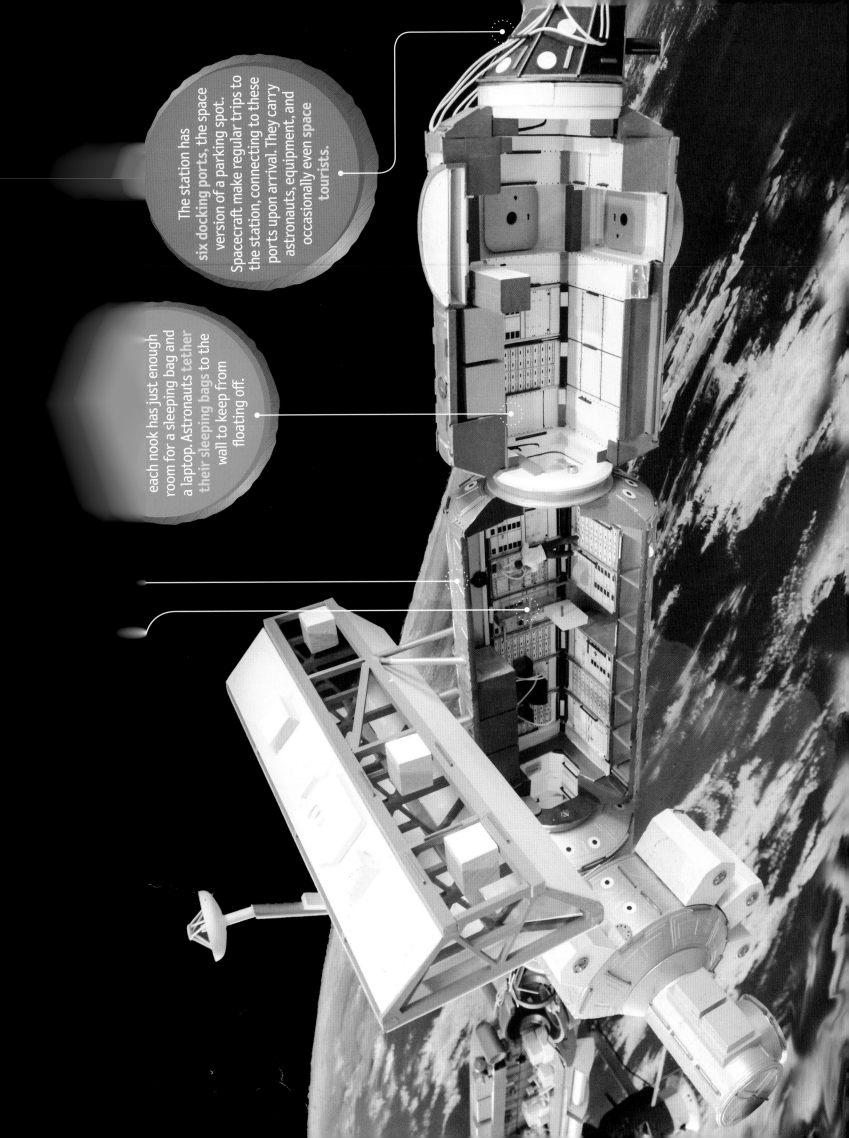

The station has **six docking ports,** the space version of a parking spot. Spacecraft make regular trips to the station, connecting to these ports upon arrival. They carry astronauts, equipment, and occasionally even space tourists.

each nook has just enough room for a sleeping bag and a laptop. Astronauts tether their sleeping bags to the wall to keep from floating off.

Crazy
CURRENCY

Check out these **STRANGE FORMS OF MONEY,** from ancient payments to **MODERN-DAY ODDITIES.**

COWRIE SHELLS

Before they were beachside souvenirs, cowrie shells were traded for goods. Ancient cultures around the world, from Africa to China, used cowries—in fact, they've been used more widely than any other form of currency ever. Native Americans also exchanged beads made from shells, called wampum. The beads took a long time to make, which made them more valuable. Talk about shelling out the cash!

PEPPERCORNS

Today it's the most widely used spice in the world. But people in the Middle Ages used peppercorns as money. In fact, demand for the spice was so high that, at one point, it was more valuable than gold. In the 1400s, there was such high demand for peppercorns that European kingdoms funded search parties for the spice.

CANDY

The city of Buenos Aires, in the South American country of Argentina, encountered a coin shortage in 2008. As a result, some stores couldn't afford to break a bill, so they demanded shoppers have exact change to pay. At other shops, in lieu of coins, businesses handed out candy to customers. Now that's a sweet deal!

RAI STONES

These stones outshine all other forms of ancient currency with their sheer size. Hundreds of years ago, limestone deposits were carved into giant stone disks and transported to the island of Yap, in the Pacific Ocean. There they became highly desired by local people. One of these heavy disks could weigh more than a car—and if a villager died while transporting a stone, the stone went up in worth.

PLAYING CARDS

When a shipment of cash was lost on its way to New France (now Canada) in the 1600s, the people awaiting its arrival had to get creative. They hatched a plan to temporarily issue playing cards until the real cash came. Once the shipment finally arrived, the cards were traded in for real money.

PARMIGIANO CHEESE

Thought cheese was just a tasty snack? A bank in Italy accepts Parmigiano cheese as collateral for unpaid loans. When a dairy farmer in the area needs money for their local cheese business, the bank gives them the cash in exchange for some of the cheese they produce. The cheese is stored in a special vault with the right conditions for it to age, so the farmers save on storage space while they work to repay their loans.

THE SECRET LIFE OF

CASH

You grab a snack at the store and walk up to the register to pay. As you **count your bills**—some old and dingy, others **crisp and new**—you accidentally **tear one** down the middle. It gets you thinking—**what happens to money** when it starts **falling apart?**

ROLLING IN THE DOUGH

First you have to know how money is made. In the United States, that's the job of the Bureau of Engraving and Printing. It prints paper money in Washington, D.C., and Fort Worth, Texas. The bills roll off the printer on big sheets of special paper, with 32 or 50 bills to a sheet. But it's not like paper we use to write on. It's a blend of cotton and linen, which makes it way more durable. (That's why it can survive a spin in the washing machine!) Then the bills are cut and distributed.

BANK OR BUST

The bureau sends its freshly printed bills to banks all over the country. The bills in your pocket started out at a bank, too. Then someone with money saved in a bank account, like a parent or grandparent, goes to withdraw some of their money. When the cash comes to you, maybe as a gift or as allowance, you take it to a store. When you go to pay, the cash goes in the register, along with the rest of the money spent at the store that day. The money eventually gets counted and taken back to the bank to be deposited in the store's account. If the bank decides any of the bills are too damaged to give out again, they set them aside to give to the Federal Reserve.

TAKING NOTES

The Federal Reserve destroys more than 5,000 tons (4,536 t) of old currency every year. The Fed uses a high-speed sorting machine to figure out if a bill is fit to stay in circulation. The Banknote Processing System 3000 scans the bills, and sensors read the notes for wear and tear and other defects like graffiti or dirt. If a bill doesn't pass the test, it gets shredded then and there. Some of the scraps end up as souvenirs for visitors to the Federal Reserve Bank of New York. Other bits are sent to companies that use them to make countertops, insulation, and other products.

Cities like Los Angeles, California, had a bright idea for the bills. The shredded bits are burned and converted into electricity to power homes and businesses. In New Orleans, Louisiana, the chopped-up cash is buried. That's because the Federal Reserve recycles it into compost that nourishes the soil for local farmers. Talk about paying it forward!

Banknote Processing System 3000

THE UNITED STATES ONCE ISSUED A $100,000 BILL.

Each of these bags of shredded currency contains about $165 worth of bills.

THE LIFE OF A BILL
Check out the average circulation of different denominations:

$1 BILLS: 3.7 YEARS
$5 BILLS: 3.4 YEARS
$10 BILLS: 3.4 YEARS
$20 BILLS: 5.1 YEARS
$50 BILLS: 12.6 YEARS
$100 BILLS: 8.9 YEARS

More **RICH** ➤
RULERS

➤ **MANSA MUSA I**
Fourteenth-century king of Timbuktu and Mali, he once controlled half of the world's gold supply.

CLEOPATRA WAS WORTH NEARLY $100 BILLION IN TODAY'S MONEY.

HOW'D THE EGYPTIAN QUEEN GET ALL THAT WEALTH?

Reigning in the first century B.C. as pharaoh of Egypt, Cleopatra controlled some of the ancient civilization's biggest industries at the time, including wheat and papyrus (an early form of paper). She even owned a perfume factory. Taking advantage of Egypt's strong economy, Cleopatra issued taxes left and right on the goods she produced, so she sometimes wound up making up to three times more than a product was worth!

For Cleopatra, being a pharaoh also meant indulging in lavish luxuries, like traveling along the Nile River on an awe-inducing ship gilded in gold. The fierce pharaoh often draped herself in pearls, and is rumored to have even swallowed one to win a bet. To prove her wealth and power, she reportedly dropped one of the world's largest known pearls into a cup of vinegar, then drank it down.

A carving of Cleopatra on a Roman temple

QUEEN ELIZABETH I
England's 16th-century ruler was responsible for creating currency using only the finest gold and silver.

KING LOUIS XIV
Nicknamed the Sun King, France's ruler made nobles spend vast amounts of money to attend his court.

WEALTH
OF
WONDERS

A journey outdoors reveals some of nature's most incredible riches. Beautiful but deadly plants twinkle in the sun to lure their next meal. Massive, magma-spewing hot spots sit preparing to erupt. Dazzling elements decorate our entire planet—and around every corner, new wonders await.

Cool
CAVES

The thought of caves stirs up a vision of **DARK, GLOOMY UNDERGROUND HOLLOWS.** But within our Earth's surface lie **SHIMMERING SIGHTS.**

CRYSTAL CAVERN
Chihuahua, Mexico

Hidden inside a limestone cavern in northwestern Mexico are gigantic glistening beams of selenite—the largest crystals the world's ever seen. This underground crystal wonderland—dubbed the Cave of the Crystals—wasn't discovered until 2000, when two brothers stumbled across the formations while drilling for lead and silver. Over hundreds of thousands of years, mineral-rich water allowed the amazing crystals to grow to larger-than-life proportions while keeping them hidden from discovery. Only after miners unknowingly drained the water in the cave were the crystals finally revealed.

NATURAL MASTERPIECE
General Carrera Lake, Chile

A serene boat ride on the turquoise waters of General Carrera Lake takes you to a peninsula made entirely of marble. Swirling shades of blue, green, and gray make up the walls of these Marble Caves. Smoothed by centuries of crashing waves, the curved walls reflect colors from the blue water below. As seasons bring changes to the lake, they are reflected in the cave overhead. In springtime, shallower water gives off a turquoise hue. But in summer, as glaciers melt and the water level rises, the water reflects a deeper blue shade.

GOLDEN GERMS
Tulelake, California, U.S.A.
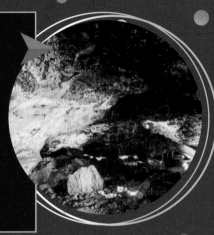

The secret to Golden Dome Cave in Lava Beds National Monument? Tiny bacteria. A colony of yellow microorganisms coat the upper region of the cave. These bacteria repel water, so drops bead up on top of the bacteria on the cave, making the dome look as though it's coated in glistening gold wallpaper.

TWINKLE, TWINKLE ...
Waitomo, New Zealand

... Little stars? No—try meat-eating worms! Lurking in these dark caves a half mile (0.8 km) underground, bioluminescent glowworm larvae twinkle like the night sky to lure their next meal. Moths, which use nature's real night sky to navigate, get confused and fly toward the glowing worms. Instead of finding their way, the moths find themselves trapped on sticky strings dangled by the worms. Once a moth gets stuck, the worm reels it in and starts to devour the slime-coated critter.

SKY'S THE LIMIT
Kamchatka Peninsula, Russia

The inside of this ice cave looks like frozen clouds that sometimes glow with a dazzling display of colorful lights. The colors come from sunlight streaming in through the cave's thin walls—or, at least, trying to. Snow and ice reflect a lot of the sunlight that reaches their surface. But some shades of light can filter through water better than others. Red and yellow tones don't make it very far through the cave's icy ceiling, but blue and violet shades do, giving this cave its unique hues.

JUMBO JACKPOTS

Eyes on the prize! Take a look at some of nature's biggest jaw-dropping jewels.

GRAND PRISMATIC SPRING

Where: Wyoming, U.S.A.

Thanks to its immense size and crazy rainbow of colors, this hot spring is a must-see stop in Yellowstone National Park. The spring is 370 feet (113 m) wide, making it the largest in the United States and the third biggest in the world. Its center, which reaches 189°F (87°C), is too hot for the heat-loving bacteria that color the water to survive, so it stays blue. But around the edges, the water cools, creating temperature rings where different-colored bacteria can thrive.

GIANT WATER LILIES

Where: South America

Forget inner tubes. Growing up to 10 feet (3 m) across, the leaves of the giant water lily (also known as lily pads) are wide enough and strong enough to support a human lying on top! The lilies grow in shallow waters along the Amazon River Basin. Thorns on their underside protect the leaves from hungry fish and other creatures swimming below.

CORPSE FLOWER ▶▶▶▶▶▶

Where: Indonesia

The world's largest single flower sort of looks more like a cartoon than an actual plant, but this rare bloom is no joke. Sometimes called a corpse flower, *Rafflesia arnoldii* stinks up the jungle with the stench of rotting flesh. The scent attracts flies and other insects, which carry off the flower's pollen to help new flowers grow. Though its smell doesn't earn it any admirers, the corpse flower was still named Indonesia's national flower.

GOLDEN NUGGET

Where: Australia

Dubbed the "Welcome Stranger," the world's biggest gold nugget was found just a few centimeters belowground. The chunk, discovered in 1869, weighed a whopping 158 pounds (72 kg). At the time, no scale could weigh something so big, so the enormous nugget had to be broken into three separate pieces. Today, only replicas of the prized find exist.

RAINBOW MOUNTAINS ⏶

Where: Gansu, China

Larger-than-life rainbows ripple across the sediment at Zhangye Danxia Landform Geological Park. The color-streaked effect comes from layers of mineral-rich sand and silt. When tectonic plates collided millions of years ago, the layers began folding and lifting to the surface, forming the Technicolor peaks.

ANGEL FALLS ⏶

Where: Venezuela

Plunging 3,212 feet (979 m)—more than twice the height of the Empire State Building—Angel Falls is the world's tallest waterfall. Setting eyes on this wondrous waterfall is all the more valuable once you know how hard it is to get there: It takes a plane trip, a river ride on a canoe, and several hours of hiking to reach the surreal spot.

BLUE STAR SAPPHIRE ⏵⏵⏵

Where: Sri Lanka

Discovered in Ratnapura—nicknamed the "City of Gems"—this rare blue stone is worth an estimated $100 million. At 1,404 carats, it's the biggest blue sapphire ever found—too big to be put in any piece of jewelry. But just like other star sapphires, the stone's surface twinkles under the light with the shape of a six-pointed star.

CHALK TOWERS

Where: Egypt

You don't expect to see much in a desert except for a blanket of sand—but the bizarre towering formations dotting Egypt's White Desert are no mirage. Made up of chalk, the massive monoliths have been shaped by harsh winds that have blown through the desert. Some of the formations' shapes have earned them laugh-worthy nicknames like "chicken" and "mushroom."

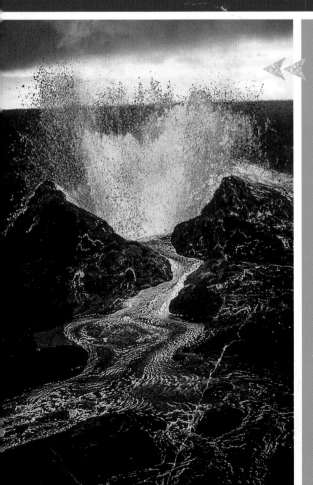

MAUNA LOA

Where: Hawaii, U.S.A.

The sheer size of this volcano is enough to blow your mind. Mauna Loa's summit reaches a staggering 13,679 feet (4,169 m) above sea level—the highest of any volcano on Earth. But aside from being the biggest, it's also one of the most active volcanoes in the world. It has erupted more than 30 times over the last 200 years, and no one knows when it might happen again!

THE WAVE

Where: Arizona, U.S.A.

You might not be able to surf here, but you'll capture some pretty cool pictures. The squiggly lines of this sandstone formation were caused by millions of years of erosion from wind and rain. The sprawling sandstone is a beautiful sight, but getting here can be dangerous: Triple-digit temperatures and twisting terrain have led some hikers to become confused and overheated.

SPOTTED LAKE

Where: British Columbia, Canada

By midsummer, when Kliluk—or Spotted Lake—has mostly evaporated, the mineral-rich water that's left behind forms pools on the lake bed. A combination of the minerals inside and the sun's reflection gives these spots their golden hues.

RICE TERRACES

Where: Banaue, Philippines

The rice paddies on the mountains of Banaue cascade down in waterfalls of green. These terraces are no accident—they're the result of farmers carefully carving into the land. The reason? So water from the rainforests above can flow down and irrigate their crops.

SHOWY

DANAKIL DEPRESSION

Where: Northern Ethiopia

It's considered one of the hottest, harshest places on Earth—but people have still found a way to live on this otherworldly desert land-scape. Scientists have studied this orange alien place to get a better understanding of how life could exist on Mars.

LAVENDER FIELDS

Where: Provence, France

Fragrant fields of lavender flowers burst onto the scene every summer. This gold mine of good-smelling purple buds is harvested and used to make soaps, perfumes, and even foods like honey and sorbet.

PANJIN RED BEACH

Where: Liaoning, China

No sand here—just a glimmering sea of crimson reeds. The plants in the Panjin wetlands turn from gorgeous green to radiant red every autumn. Hundreds of birds can be found in the area, including one that sounds quite fitting: the endangered red-crowned crane.

SPOTS

With their intense colors, these eye-catching places almost look out of this world.

GREAT BLUE HOLE

Where: Caribbean Sea, off the coast of Belize City, Belize

At the end of the last ice age, a cave system flooded and collapsed to create this giant blue abyss. Scuba divers flock to the 400-foot (122-m)-deep hole for a chance to dive through its crystal clear waters and encounter its diverse marine life, including nurse sharks and hammerheads.

LAKE HILLIER

Where: Middle Island, Australia

It looks like a giant strawberry milk shake—but this pink lake actually gets its color from salt-loving microbes. Despite its neon hue, the water's safe for swimming.

Posh POOLS

Despite its icy appearance, Pamukkale—or "cotton castle" in English—is far from frigid. Temperatures here sometimes heat up enough to reach the triple digits. Looming over a valley in Turkey's Denizli Province, the glistening bluffs hold tiers of turquoise blue waters.

HEIGHT: 325 feet (99 m)

LENGTH: 9,000 feet (2,743 m)

FIRST DISCOVERED: Around 200 B.C.

VISITORS: 1.5 million each year

Pamukkale has been a popular attraction since a king founded a town near the site.

When calcium carbonate in the water meets air, it forms a jelly-like substance that piles up as it makes its way down the cliff. Eventually the jelly dries and hardens into terraces of white limestone rock called travertine.

The water in the springs is filled with minerals, naturally occurring chemicals, and calcium carbonate (a chalklike substance).

Since its discovery, people have believed that the hot springs have healing powers.

Pamukkale has 17 hot springs, which warm water below Earth's surface. Before it spouts up into the pools, the water is heated to a toasty 95°F to 140°F (35°C to 60°C). It cools as it flows into the pools, making them like natural hot tubs.

Most corals are **CLEAR** and **COLORLESS—** they get their hues from **the billions of algae** that live inside them.

Brain Coral

Tree Coral

HOW DO CORALS BECOME BLINGED OUT WITH A RAINBOW OF COLORS?

Billions of algae live inside them—but the algae don't live rent free. Here's how it works: As larvae, corals hitch themselves to underwater rocks. Different coral species grow at different speeds, depending on their environment. As they grow, algae take up residence on the corals. By turning light from above into food (a process called photosynthesis), the algae give the coral nutrients and pigment. The amount of pigment and the species of coral determine the coral's color. No paint needed for these digs!

Cauliflower Coral

Bubblegum Coral

Bird's Nest Coral

7 Flashy FACTS About ...

NICE ICE

Not all ice is created equal. Sometimes elements align to create stunning frozen formations.

1 Extreme weather conditions cause **50-FOOT (15-m)-TALL ICE BLOCKS** to form on **RUSSIA'S LAKE BAIKAL.**

2 The world's largest ice cave can be found in the **FROZEN UNDERWORLD** of Austria's glittering **EISRIESENWELT**—German for **"WORLD OF THE ICE GIANTS."**

3 Frost flowers—**DELICATE ICE STRUCTURES** that bloom on oceans near the North and South Poles—are **HOME TO TINY MICROBES.**

4 Researchers discovered mysterious **PANCAKE-SHAPED ICE** in a Scottish lake.

5 Not all **ICEBERGS ARE WHITE** — some are **BLUE.**

6 "Ice volcanoes" **SPEW FROZEN WATER** on one of **SATURN'S MOONS.**

7 Scientists store hundreds of **ICE SAMPLES** from around the world in a **VAULT IN ANTARCTICA.**

HOT
SPOT

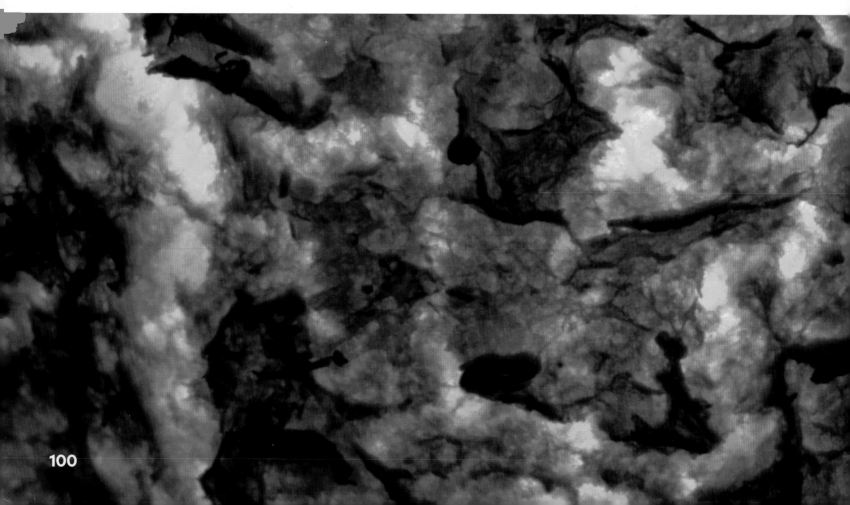

A bizarre blob of **steaming fountains bursts** with **water and color** from the barren landscape. It may look like a scene from another planet, but the surreal Fly Geyser unexpectedly **gushes up from the desert** of Nevada, U.S.A.

BIRTH OF FLY GEYSER

At first glance, Fly Geyser seems to be a natural wonder, but it's not quite natural. It's technically not a geyser either. It's an accident. Although Fly Geyser is powered by nature, it got a kick-start from humans. The 12-foot (4-m)-tall mounds spew water that continuously flows from a single underground hole, which was drilled by workers about 50 years ago. They had hoped to strike water that was so hot it could power an electrical plant with geothermal energy. The boiling water spurting from the Fly Geyser originates deep below the surface, where it is heated by shallow magma—hot, liquid rock. This wet zone is covered by a hard layer of rock, which traps the hot water. Because it can't escape as steam, the pressurized water's temperature rises far above the normal boiling point. The artificial, drilled hole gives the water a way out, like the opening of a soda bottle.

IT'S ALIVE!

Even though the water spewing from Fly Geyser tops 200°F (93°C), the temperature turned out to be too low for a geothermal plant. The hole was plugged, but the hot water eventually forced its way up. Minerals that dissolved in the exiting water gradually built the mounds and surrounding terraces. Those formations are composed of a mineral that also forms the stalagmites and stalactites in many wet limestone caverns.

Fly Geyser's mounds and terraces aren't only alive with color—they're literally alive. The brilliant reds, yellows, and greens are caused by microscopic organisms called thermophiles, or "heat lovers." They are the only life-forms that can survive in such high, deadly temperatures. Different colors of thermophiles live in water at different temperatures, creating Fly Geyser's changing colors.

HOT PURSUIT

Fly Geyser wasn't hot enough to support a geothermal plant, but it was a necessary step in a hit-or-miss process. Other heat-seeking holes in the area tapped into hotter water and were put to use. That water makes steam that cranks big machines to create electricity. Most power plants use steam, but geothermal ones don't burn coal or gas to make it, so they're much cleaner. Today, Nevada is the second largest producer of geothermal electricity in the United States. Fly Geyser may have been a miss for geothermal energy, but it sure ended up being a hit for creating a colorful new landscape.

THE NAME NEVADA COMES FROM THE SPANISH WORD FOR "SNOW-CAPPED."

Natural geysers erupt in Norris Geyser Basin in Yellowstone National Park, Wyoming, U.S.A.

Fly Geyser is covered in thermophilic algae, which is what makes the geyser so colorful.

NEVADA'S OFFICIAL STATE ANIMAL IS THE DESERT BIGHORN SHEEP.

101

Meat-eating sundew plants sparkle in the sunlight to lure their PREY.

MORE ▶
CARNIVOROUS
PLANTS

Pitcher Plant

Venus Flytrap

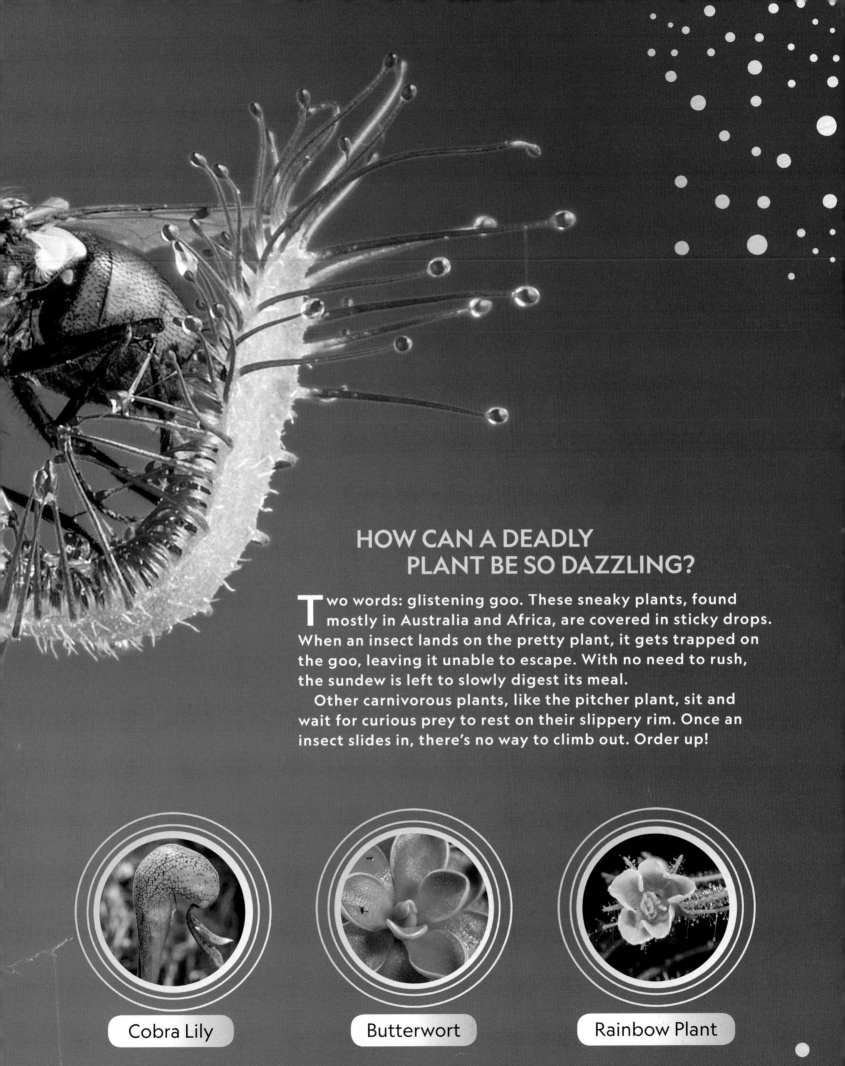

HOW CAN A DEADLY PLANT BE SO DAZZLING?

Two words: glistening goo. These sneaky plants, found mostly in Australia and Africa, are covered in sticky drops. When an insect lands on the pretty plant, it gets trapped on the goo, leaving it unable to escape. With no need to rush, the sundew is left to slowly digest its meal.

Other carnivorous plants, like the pitcher plant, sit and wait for curious prey to rest on their slippery rim. Once an insect slides in, there's no way to climb out. Order up!

Cobra Lily

Butterwort

Rainbow Plant

METALLIC
MARVELS

From striking statues and gold-covered goods to incredible iridescent animals, metallic sheens are all around us. Sometimes colorful, sometimes practical, and other times purely for show, one thing's forever true: Shimmering surfaces are always in style. But as you might guess, there's more to these lustrous looks than meets the eye.

Gallium melts in your HAND.

WHAT MAKES THE SHAPE-SHIFTING POWER POSSIBLE?

Unlike most metals, which melt at superhigh temperatures, this soft metal only needs to reach 85.6°F (29.8°C) to liquefy. Because the human body usually stays at a steady 98.6°F (37°C), a few minutes of a human's touch is all it takes to make the metal melt. It's safe to hold, but scientists always wear gloves. Liquid gallium can leave behind metallic particles on skin that can be hard to remove. Gallium also "attacks" other metals that come in contact with it—so handlers have to remove their rings before touching this melty metal.

MORE METAL MELTING POINTS

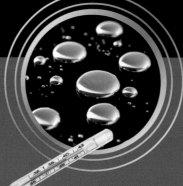

Mercury
-38°F (-39°C)

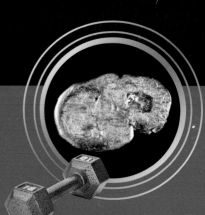

Lead
621°F (327°C)

Aluminum
1220°F (660°C)

Gold
1945°F (1063°C)

Copper
1983°F (1084°C)

Platinum
3220°F (1771°C)

Good as GOLD

FROM OUTER SPACE

protection to treatment in our bodies, get the dirt on some of gold's **STRANGEST USES.**

GLITZY GARNISH

One way to eat like a king? Try gold-dusted ice cream! Believe it or not, gold is edible. Used to garnish foods, the fancy flakes have no taste or odor. But what happens once you swallow? The human body cannot digest gold, so it just, um, passes through. You might get a stomachache if you eat too much of it, but the same could be said for ice cream.

SNOWFLAKE
Luxury Gelato

SAFE SPACE

The visors on astronaut helmets are coated with a thin layer of gold. The clever coating filters out harmful ultraviolet rays from the sun, protecting the astronauts' eyes without getting in the way of their vision. Engineers also drape gold foil over spacecraft to prevent the vehicles from overheating in outer space. Now that's cool!

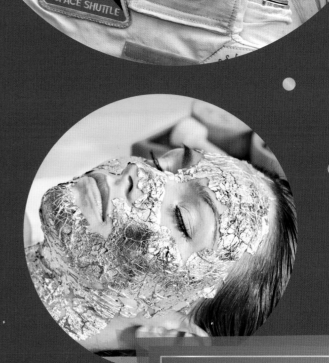

METAL MEDICINE

Gold's healing powers have been used to treat arthritis and lagophthalmos—the inability to fully shut one's eyelids. An injection of gold into the upper eyelid weighs it down, enabling it to close. Gold is also used in stents and pacemaker wires, and is even being used in specialized cancer treatments.

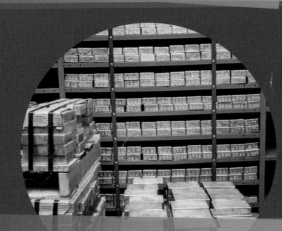

HIGH-STAKES STASH

Gold has long been used as a form of currency. Many countries today keep stashes—called gold reserves—to support their economies. The United States keeps a famous stockpile of gold bars at Fort Knox—about 4,500 tons (4,082 t), worth somewhere between $100 billion and $200 billion. The Kentucky facility stores the stash in the world's most secure vault, equipped with a 22-ton (20-t) blast-proof door and a satellite defense system that can attack from space.

FLASHY FACIAL

It's rumored that Cleopatra, queen of Egypt, slept wearing a golden mask as part of her beauty regimen. The routine supposedly preserved her flawless complexion. Today, beauty companies offer similar treatments and products promising the same results, from gold-infused serums and masks to 24-karat eye shadow.

SMILEY FACE WATER TOWER
Where: Adair, Iowa, U.S.A
Established: 1979

Nicknamed Ol' Smiley, the 250,000-gallon (946,350-L) metal water tower greets town visitors and commuters traveling along the nearby interstate highway. And it turns out the friendly tower is actually two-faced: One side smiles to the west, while the other greets the east.

STATUE OF LIBERTY
Where: New York City
Established: 1886

It took about 30 years for Lady Liberty to turn from her original brown to the green you see today. Over time, air and water reacted with the statue's copper—a process called oxidation—forming a thin layer called a patina.

BRIGHT

GOLDEN GATE BRIDGE
Where: San Francisco, California, U.S.A.
Established: 1937

The Golden Gate Bridge, made out of steel, was almost given the same colors as a bumblebee! Originally the U.S. Navy wanted to coat the overpass with black and yellow stripes to make it extra visible to sailors. Designers ultimately chose to paint the bridge "international orange," a bold orange color that would also complement the landscape.

PURPLE PEOPLE BRIDGE

Where: Newport, Kentucky, U.S.A.
Established: 1872

First opened as a railroad bridge, the Newport Southbank Bridge—popularly known as the Purple People Bridge—runs across the Ohio River, connecting Ohio and Kentucky. At 2,670 feet (814 m) long, the bridge is the longest pedestrian-only bridge in the country that connects two states.

PAINT SPLASH

Where: Sydney, Australia
Established: 2010

This sculpture adds a splash of color to the Bondi Beach coastline. The stainless steel tube, crafted for an art exhibition, points its paint explosion toward the water.

SITES

Despite their colorful facades, these eye-catching landmarks are metal at heart.

BLUE BEAR

Where: Denver, Colorado, U.S.A.
Established: 2005

The 40-foot (12-m)-tall steel-and-fiberglass bear sculpture peers into the Denver Convention Center. The artist's idea for the wild piece was rooted in nature—he was inspired by one curious bear that had been photographed peeking into the window of a local home when drought caused black bears to venture into the city.

BALLOON DOG

Where: Venice, Italy
Established: 2000

It looks like a giant balloon animal filled with air—but this hot-pink pup is made of stainless steel. The nearly 12-foot (4-m)-tall sculpture is one of five colorful versions created by artist Jeff Koons. The orange one fetched a record price of $58.4 million at auction.

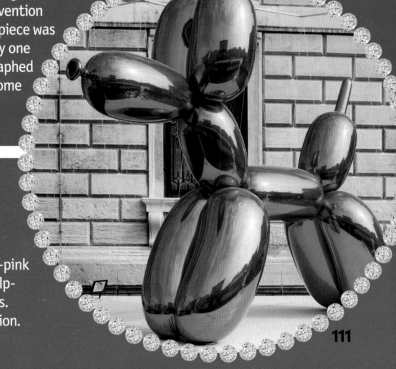

7 Flashy FACTS About ...
AMAZING ARMOR

For centuries it has protected people in battle. But armor isn't so much a uniform as it is a status symbol.

1 Some people in the **MIDDLE AGES** wore **BOILED** and **HARDENED LEATHER** for **PROTECTION.**

2 **MAIL ARMOR**—made of interlocking metal rings—took so much **MONEY AND TIME** to make, it was worn only by **WEALTHY SOLDIERS** who could afford it.

3 A **"BARD"** is **ARMOR** designed for a **HORSE.**

4 Japanese **SAMURAI** wore armor that reflected their **FAMILY'S SOCIAL STATUS.**

5 The phrase **"THROW DOWN THE GAUNTLET"** comes from the knights' tradition of tossing an armored glove to **CHALLENGE** an **OPPONENT TO A DUEL.**

6 Despite popular belief, **VIKING HELMETS** probably didn't have **HORNS.**

7 A modern-day **SUIT OF ARMOR** could cost **$10,000** or more.

113

CHAMPIONSHIP
BLING

Sporting events have their fair share of ups and downs, but these **awards have had misadventures** all their own. Unlock some of the **mysteries and mishaps** of the world's **ultimate athletic awards.**

TROPHY TURNOVER

After stealing the World Cup's Jules Rimet Trophy in 1966 just months before the big soccer tournament in England, the thief made a bold move: He sent a ransom note demanding money in exchange for the gold-plated prize. An undercover officer set out with a bag of fake bills, prepared to arrest the culprit. The officer caught the crook, but the trophy was still at large. Then an unlikely hero stepped in to save the day—a dog named Pickles, who sniffed out the soccer swag on one of his daily walks. The trophy was recovered just in time to be awarded at the World Cup as planned, making this find a big victory.

Bad luck struck again in 1983, when the trophy was lifted once more, this time in Brazil. To this day it hasn't been recovered, but it's rumored to have been melted down into metal bars. Thankfully, another trophy was made after the first robbery—and the prize got an upgrade. The new and improved trophy, still used today, is made of 18-karat solid gold.

LOST POSSESSION

They're the most sought-after prizes in American football. Awarded to each member of the winning Super Bowl team, one of these championship rings can cost as much as $36,500—more than the price of a car!—to create. Each ring is usually made of gold and bedazzled with precious stones, sometimes numbering in the hundreds.

John Schmitt, starting center for the New York Jets, won his revered ring in 1969. A few years after the big win, while out for a swim on a vacation in Hawaii, the ring slipped off his finger. When he got back to the beach and noticed the ring was gone, he swam back in, but he had no luck retrieving the bling.

Little did he know, all hope was not lost. Years later, a lifeguard found the ring and stashed it away. When the lifeguard died, his great-niece took the ring to a jeweler and discovered it was the real deal. She returned it to John—more than 40 years after it was lost. That's one epic recovery.

ON THIN ICE

The world-famous Stanley Cup—named after Lord Stanley of Preston, the 1892 governor general of Canada—is awarded each year to the winners of the National Hockey League's playoff game. Lord Stanley, a big hockey fan, brought back the original silver cup—which now tops the trophy—from a trip to London.

When the Montreal Canadiens won the Stanley Cup in 1924, naturally they wanted to take the trophy with them to a celebratory dinner at the team owner's house. Team members hit a snag when they got a flat tire on their way to the party. To get to the spare tire in the trunk, first they had to take out the coveted cup. They changed the tire and quickly got on their way—but left the trophy on the side of the road! Thankfully, when they doubled back, it was right where they'd left it. Nowadays each player on the winning team gets to spend a day with the cup—but with a chaperone nearby, just in case.

A French player holds the FIFA 2018 World Cup trophy aloft after their win over Croatia.

WINNERS OF THE INDIANAPOLIS 500 AUTO RACE GET THEIR FACES SCULPTED ON THE BORG-WARNER TROPHY.

Washington Capitals hockey player Alexander Ovechkin raises the Stanley Cup trophy high after the team's 2018 playoff win.

WINNING TEAM ROSTERS HAVE BEEN ENGRAVED INTO THE STANLEY CUP TROPHY SINCE THE EARLY 1900S.

Super Bowl championship rings can be adorned with hundreds of precious stones.

More NATURE-Inspired TECH

CHEETAH BOT

The cheetah inspired this robot, which runs and leaps over obstacles.

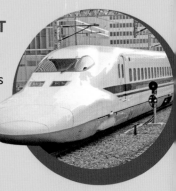

STEEL-FRAMED "SUPERTREES" IN SINGAPORE HARNESS SOLAR POWER.

COULD THESE TOWERING STRUCTURES BE THE FUTURE FOR TREES?

It's definitely an idea with room to grow. The human-made forest includes 18 artificial trees, each towering somewhere between 80 and 160 feet (25 and 50 m) above the urban landscape. Fitted with solar cells, some of these super-trees capture the sun's energy and use it to generate power that provides light and helps water flow to places it's needed below.

Tropical flowers and ferns climb around the trees' steel framework, and the canopies that fan out help moderate temperatures and provide shelter to visitors underneath. This tech is really branching out!

SHINKANSEN BULLET TRAIN
To reduce noise, this train's nose resembles the beak of the stealthy kingfisher.

WINGSUIT
These sky-high suits mimic the skin flaps on flying squirrels.

SPACE ROBOTS
The gripping feet of geckos sparked the idea for a bot that could grab space trash.

INCREDIBLE
IRIDESCENCE

Unlike other colorful creatures, iridescent animals don't get their gorgeous hues from pigments in their feathers or skin—they get them from the way light reflects off their bodies. The magnificent metallic colors act like optical illusions, seeming to change as light shifts to different angles.

FIERY-THROATED HUMMINGBIRD ▶▶▶ ▶▶

Lives in: Costa Rica and Panama

In the right light, this fiery flier's full range of colors is on display. This vibrant bird lives high in the cloud forests of Costa Rica and Panama, where it has a reputation for being very territorial. The hummingbird's plumage is most colorful when seen straight on, which intimidates intruders that attempt to face off.

BOESEMAN'S RAINBOWFISH ▲

Lives in: Ayamaru Lakes, Indonesia

This fancy fish shines in its freshwater habitats with an amazing variety of colorful, shimmering scales. The Boeseman's rainbowfish is a standout among the group, with males' bodies transitioning from a bright bluish gray head to a deep orange color toward its back. Though one would be stunning enough, these friendly fish like to travel in packs. If left alone, a rainbowfish might get stressed and lose its luster.

CRYSTAL LOBSTER

Lives in: Atlantic coast of North America

Some of the rarest in the lobster world, the albino or "crystal" lobster is not an easy find. The odds of seeing one of these sea creatures is one in 100 million. Even so, a handful have been spotted in the waters around Maine, U.S.A., in recent years.

BRAZILIAN RAINBOW BOA

Lives in: Northern South America

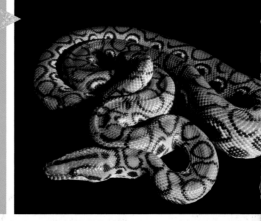

This sleek snake is well suited to its name. On top of its red, orange, and brown body, iridescent structures on the reptile's scales dazzle with a spectrum of colorful shades when light shines across them. Because the structures are on top of the scales, instead of under the skin like with other animals, the iridescent pattern is especially noticeable after the snake sheds.

BLUE MORPHO BUTTERFLY

Lives in: Mexico, Central and South America

The butterfly's wings are blinged out with millions of tiny scales that diffract light, giving off a dazzling blue hue. When the insect flies, it looks like it's flashing across the sky. But a hungry bird passing by the butterfly might miss it. How? The undersides of its wings are dull and brown, helping the butterfly hide from predators.

119

METALLIC SWEAT BEE

Lives in: Canada to Argentina

Metallic sweat bees have style and skill. You probably know some bees make honey, and some can pack a painful sting. But what you might not realize is these buzzers are talented pollen transporters. Thanks to "pollen baskets"—which are more like hair-lined grooves—on their back legs, they're able to make off with stockpiles of the prized powder. Transporting the pollen means it can be introduced to other plants, and when mixed with another plant's pollen, combines to help make new plants.

VIOLET-BACKED STARLING ⟩⟩⟩⟩⟩

Lives in: Africa, Saudi Arabia, and Yemen

Also known as the amethyst starling, this bird is a real gem. The male starlings are the lucky ones that get the incredible purple plumage. Females, on the other hand, are mostly brown with a white-specked stomach.

CARIBBEAN REEF SQUID ≫≫≫≫ ≫≫

Lives in: Atlantic Ocean and Caribbean Sea

According to scientists, squid control the shimmer of their "electric" skin through their nervous system. The squid can instantly change its color and brightness to give off the appearance it wants. Scientists still aren't sure how the squid chooses its shades. What's even more puzzling: why a color-blind creature like a squid would need to change colors at all.

◀ RAINBOW SCARAB

Lives in: United States

These metallic, emerald-hued beetles live in poop all their lives. The dung beetles are drawn to the droppings of bison, which once roamed North America by the millions. The beetles consume the bison poop and help maintain the soil quality of the plains where they're found.

GOLDEN MOLE ≫≫≫≫≫≫≫

Lives in: Southern Africa

Golden moles are blind, spending most of their time in dark burrows belowground. Most animals use their iridescence to attract mates, but with such dark homes, their flashy fur doesn't really help. So if not to catch the eye of other golden moles, why have such shiny hair? According to one study, it serves another purpose. The flattened hairs on these animals act to repel water and help the moles glide more easily through dirt and sand. The hairs' flat surface means more area to reflect light. Now that's a smooth move.

Medal MADNESS

They're at the pinnacle of athletic prowess. At the modern Olympic Games, athletes from around the world bring their A game in the hopes of being rewarded with one of the sporting world's most renowned medals. Over the years medal creators have even, well, meddled with some of the ingredients to make the coveted prizes truly irreplaceable.

SOME SILVER MEDALS FOR THE 2016 SUMMER GAMES IN RIO DE JANEIRO, BRAZIL, HAD PIECES OF RECYCLED MIRRORS INSIDE.

AT ANCIENT OLYMPIC GAMES, WINNERS WERE AWARDED CROWNS CRAFTED FROM OLIVE BRANCHES.

TEN GOLD MEDALS AT THE 2014 WINTER GAMES IN SOCHI, RUSSIA, CONTAINED PIECES OF A MASSIVE METEORITE.

FOR THE 2000 SUMMER OLYMPICS IN SYDNEY, AUSTRALIA, BRONZE MEDALS WERE MADE FROM RECYCLED COINS.

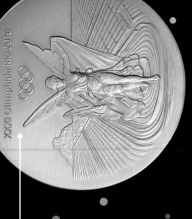

Third-place bronze burst onto the Olympic scene in 1904. Studies today show bronze medalists are actually happier than their second-place silver competitors. The reason? Researchers think that while silver medalists are secretly sad they missed out on winning gold, bronze medalists are pleased they placed at all.

At the first modern Olympics, held in 1896, silver was supreme. First-place winners received silver medals, while second place got copper, and third place—sadly—got nothing. At the 1900 Olympics, winners didn't get medals at all—instead they were awarded paintings! Silver took a backseat to gold starting with the 1904 Olympic Games.

Despite the Olympics being a Greek tradition, for more than 70 years the stadium on the medals' fronts erroneously showed the Colosseum in Rome, Italy. In 2004 it was corrected to show the Panathenaic Stadium in Athens, Greece.

You might expect this first-place prize to pack a hefty price tag—but that's not the case. Nowadays "gold" medals are more than 90 percent silver, making them worth only a few hundred dollars. There actually hasn't been a solid gold medal since 1912. If they were nothing but gold today, they'd probably be worth more like $75,000.

Nike, the winged goddess of victory (and the shoe company's namesake), is front and center on each medal.

CHAPTER 7

SUPER SPLURGES

What would you buy if you had an endless stash of cash? Maybe a mansion, or a private jet, or a lifetime supply of ice cream? When it comes to wild expenditures, some buys might make you green with envy, while others are just plain mind-boggling.

Climbing Mount Everest can cost more than buying a HOUSE.

GEAR UP ▶

Here are some items you'd need to make the climb.

Oxygen Canister

Ice Axe

WHERE DOES ALL THAT MONEY GO?

Guides and Sherpas willing to risk their lives to accompany a climber will charge a whopping $65,000 a trip. Then there's the permit, which starts at $10,000. And don't forget special equipment so you don't freeze. Add it all up and a trip up the famed peak can run you $100,000 or more. Guess that's what you'd call a steep price.

Crampons

Goggles

Water Purifier

High-Style
HOTELS

With **ACCOMMODATIONS** like these, who would ever want to **CHECK OUT?**

DEEP DIGS

Rangali Island, Maldives

Eat and sleep 16 feet (5 m) below the surface of the Indian Ocean at this incredible island retreat. Guests at the Conrad Maldives can take in the serene scene of sea creatures swimming overhead in both the resort's restaurant and its two-story private villa. Who needs to count sheep when you can count fish?

FIT FOR A KING
Liaoning, China

It's hard not to feel like royalty during an overnight stay at this palatial spot. The Castle Hotel towers over the trees of Lotus Mountain in China's northeastern city of Dalian. Guests here can unwind while enjoying high tea in the lobby lounge, or visit the heated indoor swimming pool overlooking the ocean nearby. Talk about a lap of luxury.

ROCK-STAR STAY
Around the World

Guests at the world's Hard Rock Hotels can rock around the clock like real-life stars. Premium Fender guitars are ready to be reserved for in-room jam sessions throughout a guest's stay. Beginners can even get in-room video lessons to take their rocking to the next level.

DISCO TREE HOUSE
Harads, Sweden

The Mirrorcube at Sweden's Treehotel is a supreme forest hideaway. Inside the camouflaged cube is a bed, toilet, lounge, and rooftop terrace. Built on an aluminum frame, the cube's glass walls reflect the forest surroundings. They're covered in an infrared film whose color is invisible to the human eye but can be seen by birds, serving as a warning to keep them from flying into the cube.

INCREDIBLE IGLOOS
Saariselkä, Finland

Want to sleep under the stars? Well, at Kakslauttanen, a resort located above the Arctic Circle in Finland, you can! These glass-domed igloos are perfect for viewing the spectacular colors of the northern lights and the shining stars of the Arctic sky.

7 Flashy FACTS About ...

BIG-TICKET TRAVEL

The sky-high costs of these transportation methods will boggle your brain.

1 A businessman dropped **$4.8 BILLION** to sail a **PLATINUM-AND-GOLD YACHT,** which came with art made from **T. REX BONES** and meteors.

2 Some **PARKING SPACES** in New York City **COST $1 MILLION.**

3 You can't actually **RIDE IT,** but that didn't stop someone from designing a **$15,000 GOLD-PLATED SKATEBOARD.**

4

For **$1.5 MILLION,** a department store sells private planes **COATED IN ROSE GOLD.**

5

A two-week stay in an imperial suite on one **TRANS-SIBERIAN RAILWAY TRAIN** would set you back more than **$25,000.**

6

Studded with **600 SWAROVSKI CRYSTALS,** a limited-edition **GOLD-PLATED** bike cost **$100,000.**

7

The **WORLD'S MOST EXPENSIVE CAR,** a silver Ferrari, sold in 2018 for **$70 MILLION.**

GOLDEN SUSHI

Why eat sushi wrapped in seaweed when you can have it wrapped in 24-karat gold? Some restaurants around the world have taken sushi to the next level by rolling it in thin sheets of edible gold, with some rolls fetching nearly $100.

VALUABLE VEGGIES

Asparagus-like hop shoots emerge for only a short time each spring, making them a rare commodity. Sometimes costing $600 a pound, they're considered by some people to be the most expensive vegetable in the world.

EXPENSIVE

MELON MANIA

These rare cantaloupes, dubbed Yubari King melons, get their name from the Japanese town where they grow in small numbers. Often sold in twos, they usually run about $50 to $100—but people have paid as much as $26,000 for a pair of these prized fruits.

GRATUITOUS GRAPES

Thirty juicy Ruby Roman grapes nabbed $11,000 at an auction in Japan, where purchasing high-priced fruit is often seen as a status symbol. That's about $360 a pop.

FANCY FRUITCAKE

This is not your average fruitcake. Studded with 223 diamonds, this two-layer cake rang in at $1.72 million. Created for display in a Japanese department store, the sweet master-piece took six months to design, and another month to make.

EATS

This rainbow buffet is fit for those with expensive taste ... literally.

BILBERRY BONANZA

Packed with more healthy nutrients than blueberries, these European fruits are in high demand worldwide. In just one decade, Finland tripled its exports of this prized berry, earning an eye-popping $370 million.

HIGH-PRICED SPICE

At $2,000 a pound, saffron is the world's most expensive spice. Grown from the saffron crocus flower, about 210,000 dried stig-mas (there are only three per flower) have to be picked by hand to make a single pound of saffron.

BLOCKBUSTER
BLING

It's no spoiler: **The film industry rakes in billions of dollars** at the box office each year. Creators spend big bucks to make a blockbuster movie—sometimes more than **$100 million!** That hefty price tag covers everything from **paying the actors** to **building the sets** to—yes—even getting the right props.

FOLLOWING THE HEART

When it came to the famed diamond necklace in *Titanic*, one of the biggest moneymaking movies of all time, creators turned to history for inspiration. The Heart of the Ocean featured a rare blue diamond, loosely based on the Hope Diamond. But the real-life stone was actually a sapphire, and the necklace was called the Love of the Sea. Although the real bling wasn't worn by French royalty, like in the movie, it did strike a similarity with one major plot point: The Love of the Sea was given to a woman aboard the R.M.S. *Titanic* by her travel companion as they were setting sail together for a new life.

The original necklace, seen throughout the film, is made of inexpensive stones and belongs to a private collector. But another version, never used in the film, is a heart-shaped blue sapphire totaling 171 carats, surrounded by 103 diamonds and set in platinum. The stunning piece was purchased at a charity auction for an equally stunning $2.2 million.

A QUICK SABER

Some film companies spend megabucks on their movie props. In other cases, props start out with not much value at all—but if the film's a hit, the props may wind up being worth a good chunk of change. Take the lightsaber Luke Skywalker used in two *Star Wars* movies. Despite costing next to nothing to make, the saber became so iconic

that, when it went up for auction in 2008, it sold for $240,000—proving that one person's trash really can be another person's treasure.

NO PLACE LIKE HOME

Props can gain such notoriety that people go to great lengths to have them—even going so far as to steal. That's what happened to a pair of ruby slippers from *The Wizard of Oz*. Several pairs were made for the movie, including one set that ended up at a Minnesota, U.S.A., museum. In 2005 a thief stole the slippers, prompting the owner to put up a $1 million reward for their return.

Not only did someone offer a huge sum to get their slippers back—other owners requested big bucks to preserve their shoe specimens. In 2016 the Smithsonian Institution launched a fund-raising campaign to preserve its prized pair of Dorothy's ruby slippers. The $350,000 raised was enough to repair the shoes' materials and build a special temperature-controlled case for them. Now these shoes are sitting pretty.

The real Love of the Sea necklace

JAMES CAMERON'S 1997 FILM *TITANIC* IS ONE OF THE BIGGEST MONEYMAKING MOVIES OF ALL TIME. TO DATE IT'S MADE MORE THAN $2 BILLION.

DOROTHY'S SLIPPERS IN *THE WIZARD OF OZ* WERE ORIGINALLY SILVER—BUT FILM-MAKERS MADE THEM RED SO THEY'D STAND OUT ON SCREEN.

Luke Skywalker with a lightsaber

Awesome
ABODES

Big or small, these houses **ROCK THE BLOCK.**
The owners of these **POSH PADS** are surely living large.

MILLION-DOLLAR DOLLHOUSE

This mini mansion would delight any doll, with seven stories, 29 rooms, and secret passageways throughout. Up top, a "wizard's tower" comes complete with tiny telescopes. Artists from around the world contributed teensy tapestries, custom chandeliers, and other unique handcrafted pieces for the home. It took a whopping 13 years to complete this $8.5 million miniature castle, which even has running water and electricity.

GINGERBREAD GLITZ

For the price of a real residence, one company created the ultimate edible home. Listed at $78,000, the gingerbread house used premium ingredients, which didn't stop with the toppings. Instead of licorice and gumdrops, this extravagant pad was adorned with 150 pearls and a five-carat ruby. That's one sweet spot.

PORCELAIN PAD

Here's a house that took "deck the halls" literally. China's Porcelain House is covered with ancient ceramic vases, plates, and bowls, and more than 400 million ancient ceramic chips. The pad, now a museum, holds hundreds of stone carvings and 20 tons (18 t) of crystals and agates. With historic treasures lining the walls, this house is truly priceless.

CURVY CASA

This surreal spot in Barcelona, Spain, is like something out of a strange dream. Named Casa Batlló, the internationally renowned building was designed by architect Antoni Gaudí. Locals call it the House of Bones, and for good reason—the balconies are decorated with railings that resemble giant skulls. The roof is dubbed the "dragon's back" for its shape and shiny "scales" that change color as you move.

MARBLE MANSION

Built for the wealthy Vanderbilt family in the late 1800s, Marble House in Newport, Rhode Island, U.S.A., was a gift from Mr. Vanderbilt to his wife for her 39th birthday. At the time, the 52-room home reportedly cost a total of $11 million to construct, which included $7 million for the marble alone. (That total today? More than $270 million!) The home's "Gold Room" is the epitome of opulence, dazzling visitors with walls covered in 24-karat gold leaf.

Over-the-Top TOY

This teddy's eyes are made of two sapphires surrounded by rhinestones and rimmed with gold.

Sparkling sapphire eyes and a body of gold make this teddy bear a standout stuffed animal.

Only 125 of these teddy bears were ever produced.

A medallion around the bear's neck commemorates the toy company's 125-year history.

The blinged-out bear is paired with a toy elephant in a saddle bedazzled with onyx and rhinestones.

Gold threads glitter among the fine mohair (hair from an angora goat) and silk that make up the bear's fur.

Its mouth and nose are stitched with 24-karat gold.

The first teddy bear was created in 1902 in honor of then President Theodore Roosevelt.

FLASHY FESTIVALS

These traditions aren't just rich in culture. Some spirited celebrants pull out all the stops for these spectacular events.

WHITE NIGHTS
Where: St. Petersburg, Russia

For two months of the year, nighttime in St. Petersburg is almost nonexistent. Thanks to the city's position on the globe, the sun's out nearly 24/7 between late May and July. The main event celebrates the end of the school year with a night of fancy fireworks, concerts, and the sailing of scarlet-colored ships.

HOLI
Where: India

Known as the festival of colors, this Hindu celebration is a blast—literally. Marked by throwing bright neon powder, Holi celebrates the end of winter. The colors carry meaning—red, for example, stands for love, while green means new beginnings. Bonfires, sweets, and dancing are also parts of this bright bash.

NEW YEAR'S FIREWORKS ⟫⟫⟫⟫⟫⟫

Where: Dubai, United Arab Emirates

It should come as no surprise that the city with the world's tallest building marks the new year with one of the world's biggest fireworks displays. In 2014 the show broke a world record for the largest ever display, using close to 480,000 fireworks shells in just six minutes (that's about 1,300 fireworks a second!).

CARNIVAL

Where: Rio de Janeiro, Brazil

Samba dancers dress to impress during this wild event. Their outfits, often adorned with sequins, feathers, and jewels, are typically crafted by hand. Being chosen to ride on one of the parade's equally extravagant floats is a huge honor, and some dancers spend as much as $10,000 on a rocking costume.

FESTIVAL OF THE SUN
Where: Cusco, Peru

In ancient times, the Inca celebrated the winter solstice and the sun god Inti with dances, parades, and lavish feasts. Today Peruvians re-create parts of the ceremony with a parade through Cusco. The guest of honor? The Inca ruler, or Sapa Inca, who's lifted through the streets on a golden throne.

CHIANG MAI FLOWER FESTIVAL
Where: Thailand

Each February Thailand explodes with colorful blooms for this funky festival. Carefully crafted flower-covered floats shaped like animals and other symbols take over the city of Chiang Mai. The location is fitting: the Thai town is commonly called the "Rose of the North."

DAY OF THE DEAD

Where: Mexico

During Día de los Muertos, or Day of the Dead, loved ones gather for parades, visit cemeteries, and decorate *ofrendas*, or altars, to celebrate the dearly departed. And while splurging isn't required, some altars offer up elaborate dishes or fancy goods, making this a pricey presentation.

LAS FALLAS

Where: Valencia, Spain

The city of Valencia is literally ablaze during this national festival. Revelers set fire to hundreds of huge, cartoon-like puppets in the streets to celebrate Saint Joseph, the patron saint of carpenters. One of these puppets, or *ninots*, can cost more than $100,000 to create.

SPLENDID
SCIENCE

Thanks to scientists, we have a wealth of knowledge about our sparkling world. Science has helped us know how to spot a fake pearl, why some animals change colors ... even where to find diamonds in space. The value of all this info? Pretty much priceless.

Sea sapphires shimmer one second, then are INVISIBLE the next.

HOW DO THEY PULL OFF THE DISAPPEARING ACT?

The secret to the ant-size sea creature's shine lies between layers of crystal plates inside their bodies. Here, the thickness of their cells' material determines the sea sapphire's color, from radiant red to brilliant blue to glistening gold. When light bounces off the cells at the right angle, it's reflected—giving off vivid flashes of color. As the sea sapphire swims and the angle of light shifts, the tricky creature seemingly disappears into the water.

Only males pull off this optical illusion. As to why sea sapphires shimmer, scientists aren't really sure. Some possible reasons? They might be avoiding predators, or they could be trying to attract mates. How's that for a magical moment?

MORE SHINY ▶
SEA CREATURES

Moon Jellyfish

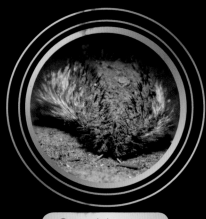
Sea Mouse

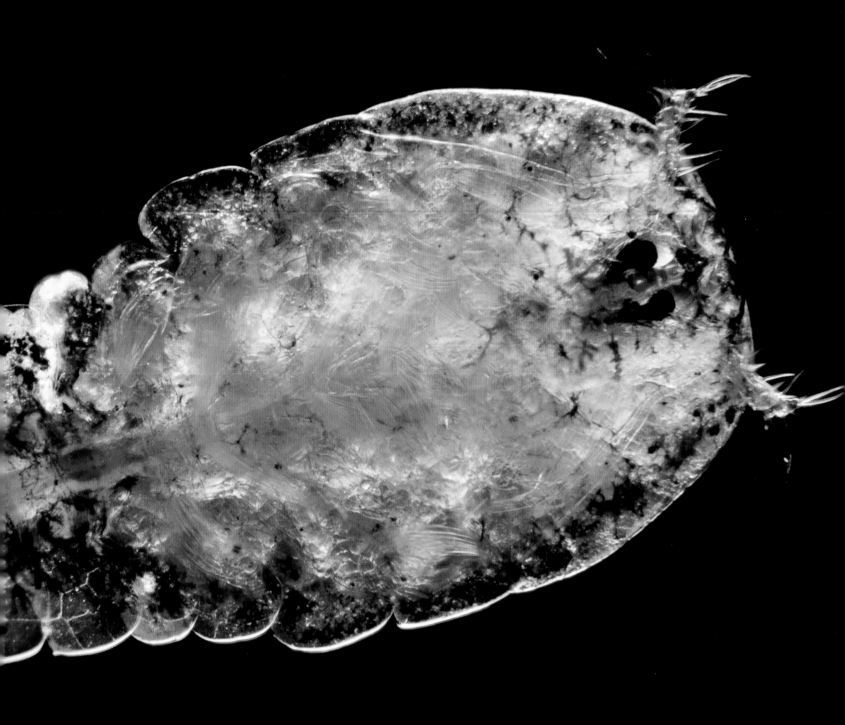

Firefly Squid

Clusterwink Snail

Comb Jelly

Real or FAKE?

Don't be fooled. Here are some **TRIED-AND-TRUE WAYS TO TEST** whether or not you've got **REAL RICHES ON YOUR HANDS**—no science lab required.

Fake

DIAMONDS OR DUDS?
A cubic zirconia, sometimes called a CZ, is a crystalline material that looks a lot like a diamond. The easiest way to tell a diamond from an imposter like a CZ is the fog test. Breathe a puff of air on the diamond in question. If the fog disappears right away, it's probably a diamond. But if it takes longer, you might have a CZ on your hands. Fog doesn't show up on diamonds because the stones are so good at conducting heat that it evaporates instantly.

PROPER PEARLS

People have come up with creative ways to imitate pearls, whether it's with painted beads or waxed glass. One way to put a pearl to the test, believe it or not, is with your teeth. Gently rub the pearl against your tooth. If it's real, the pearl will feel gritty. Fingernails work too. If you produce a bit of powder from scratching the pearl, it's real. Touching it again should make the scratch disappear.

Fake

BRILLIANT BILLS

Want to make sure that a $100 bill is the real deal? The newest U.S. hundreds have a lot of features to distinguish them from counterfeits. Hold the note to the light and you can see a vertical thread, which glows pink under ultraviolet light. Move the bill back and forth and a blue ribbon woven into the bill changes its imagery from bells to "100s." As it moves, you can also see color-shifting ink on parts of the bill that go from copper to green.

Real

SERIOUS SILVER

If you've got a big chunk of silver, consider the ice test. Head to the freezer and grab an ice cube. Put it on top of the metal, then keep your eyes on its reaction. If the ice starts to melt immediately, it's probably real silver. That's because real silver conducts heat way better than fakes, which might melt the ice slowly, or not at all.

Real

Real

GOT GOLD?

Grab a superstrong magnet (your standard refrigerator magnet won't quite do the trick) and put it up to the gold. Gold itself is not magnetic, so it won't be attracted to the magnet. Don't have a magnet on hand? Another way to tell if you've got fake gold is by wearing it around for a while. If your skin turns black or green where the metal touched it, then it's fake.

Perfect PEARLS

Ancient Greeks believed pearls were the hardened tears from Aphrodite, the goddess of love. The truth? Pearls grow from pesky particles that find their way inside mollusks. Here's how a mollusk creates one of these lustrous gems.

- **AVERAGE TIME TO FORM: At least six months**
- **GROWN IN: Oysters, mussels, and clams**
- **FOUND IN: Freshwater and saltwater**

1 A pearl starts as an invasive particle—like a parasite, stray bit of food, or a grain of sand—inside a mollusk.

2 The particle irritates the mollusk, so its mantle forms a sac to surround the foreign intruder.

3 The particle makes its way past the mollusk's shell.

4 The mollusk secretes layers of nacre, or pearl, that cover the sac.

5 Eventually the particle becomes a fully formed pearl.

PRIZED PEARL

After keeping it hidden under his bed for 10 years, a fisherman made a splash in 2016 when he revealed what many now say is the world's largest natural pearl ever found.

FOUND IN:
The Philippines

WEIGHT:
75 pounds (34 kg)

DIMENSIONS:
26 inches by 12 inches (66 cm by 30 cm)

POTENTIAL WORTH:
$100 million

COLOR-CHANGING CREATURES

By studying these animals, researchers have revealed the science behind their amazing abilities to change hues.

GOLDEN TORTOISE BEETLE

Lives in: North and South America

Look quickly at a golden tortoise beetle on a leaf and you might think you're just seeing a drop of dew. But bump into the branch holding that leaf and you'll see a stunning change. When disturbed, the color under a golden tortoise beetle's hard, transparent shell goes from a metallic sheen to a bright yellow or red color with black spots. Scientists aren't totally sure why the beetle does this. One theory suggests it's to make birds think twice about eating the insects because the spotted pattern mimics a ladybug, which birds don't like to taste.

PANTHER CHAMELEON

Lives in: Madagascar

The panther chameleon is a master quick-change artist. The reptile owes some of its spectacular color-changing capabilities to a surprising source: tiny built-in crystals. Embedded in its skin are layers of crystallized cells, which help the chameleon change color. When the chameleon relaxes these cells, light reflects in a way that makes it look blue. When the cells are stretched, the reptile looks yellow or red.

RIBBON EEL

Lives in: Indian and Pacific Oceans

These sea creatures don't just change color—they can change their gender, too. All ribbon eels are born male. When they're young, the eels are mostly black. Adults that stay male become a brilliant blue with a yellow mouth and fin, but those that become females transform into an electric yellow.

PYGMY SEAHORSE
Lives in: Pacific Ocean

Searching for a pygmy seahorse is like playing hide-and-seek underwater. The 0.8-inch (2-cm) seahorses are so skilled at blending their bodies' color and texture among vibrant corals that the first species wasn't discovered until 1969. Several more species were only recently discovered in 2009—and there could still be more!

ARCTIC FOX

Lives in: Europe and North America

When we're pulling out our warm winter jackets, the arctic fox is putting on its own winter coat. In warmer months, the fox's fur is thin and brown to match the ground, but when the weather gets colder and snow starts to fall, the fox grows a thicker coat to stay hidden and warm.

PEACOCK FLOUNDER ⟫⟫⟫⟫⟫

Lives in: Atlantic Ocean

Unlike the elaborately feathered peacock, the peacock flounder is great at going unseen. Using both eyes on one side of its body, the fish looks around the ocean and sends a message to its specialized skin cells, which match their pigments to the fish's surroundings. The flattened fish spends a lot of its time on the ocean floor, where it can bury its camouflaged body in sand and keep both eyes out for predators.

154

BLUE-RINGED OCTOPUS

Lives in: Indian and Pacific Oceans

This tiny palm-size creature is cute, but deadly. The gold-colored octopus shows its brilliant blue rings only when it feels threatened, giving predators a clear warning sign to stay away. If the predators don't comply, the octopus might deliver a lethal bite, injecting toxic venom a thousand times more potent than cyanide.

FROGFISH

Lives in: Oceans around the world

Before scientists knew frogfish changed colors, fish with different shades were classified as different species. Nowadays scientists know these creepy fish change color to match what's in their habitat. But the color change isn't quick—it can take days or weeks for the frogfish to adjust its hue.

CRAB SPIDER

Lives in: North America

In its white form, the goldenrod crab spider would be easy to spot on a bright yellow flower. So, to stay hidden while it waits for prey to pass by, this arachnid changes color to match its background. Once it blends in, the spider can sneak up and grab its prey with its front legs, then use its venomous fangs to paralyze prey before chowing down.

7 Flashy FACTS About ...
SPARKLING SPACE

Not everything that glitters comes from our planet—scientists have spotted some awesome otherworldly things in our universe.

1 Meteorites called **PALLASITES** contain glimmering bits of **PERIDOT CRYSTALS.**

2 **MOON ROCKS** have rained down to Earth after being **EJECTED** from the **MOON'S SURFACE.**

3 Researchers discovered **OPAL DEPOSITS** on Mars.

4 NASA scientists discovered **QUARTZ-LIKE CRYSTALS** that form clouds **AROUND STARS.**

A cristobalite crystal in space

5 Storms of solid **DIAMONDS SWIRL** around the cores of **URANUS** and **NEPTUNE.**

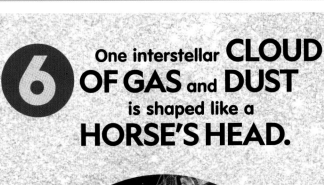

6 One interstellar **CLOUD OF GAS** and **DUST** is shaped like a **HORSE'S HEAD.**

7 If **METALS TOUCH** in space, they're **STUCK TOGETHER FOREVER.**

DISCO BALL VS. SOCCER BALL

SEE For YOURSELF ➤
TAKE THE TEST!
For each matchup, pick the item you like better.

HUMANS MAY BE DRAWN TO SHINY THINGS BECAUSE THEY REMIND US OF OUR NEED FOR WATER.

FEELING THIRSTY?

That could be because, according to one study, seeing a shiny object triggers our built-in desire to stay hydrated. Researchers came to this conclusion after splitting study participants into three groups, based on their level of thirst. One group was given crackers, another crackers and water, and a third got nothing. Then they showed the participants photos on glossy paper and nonglossy paper. The thirstier the person, the more they preferred the glossy photos.

THE BEAN IN CHICAGO, ILLINOIS, U.S.A. VS. KIDNEY BEANS

MARBLES VS. ROCKS

DID YOU GO FOR THE SHINY ITEMS? **MIGHT BE TIME FOR A GLASS OF WATER!**

CHEERY

Yellow brings a sense of warmth and happiness. But it doesn't make everybody happy—babies tend to cry more in yellow rooms than in rooms painted other colors. Maybe it's because yellow has also been shown to increase metabolism (making you hungry faster) and to cause our eyes to get tired.

HEALTHY >

Green reminds us of tranquility and nature. Green spaces are said to be more calming, and the color has even been shown to have stress-relieving effects. People reportedly get fewer stomachaches when in green areas, which might be why performers wait in "green rooms" before going on stage.

COLOR DE

ENERGIZED

The color orange can drum up excitement, which might be why so many sports teams use it as one of their colors. Orange is also an attention-grabber, which is why everything from traffic cones to public advertisements use the color. Researchers say seeing orange can even increase one's oxygen supply to the brain.

COURAGEOUS

Purple encourages creativity and portrays wisdom. And when it comes to colors we can see, it's also got the most powerful wavelength, which might explain why it's often linked to cosmic and supernatural forces.

EXCITED

Red is the classic color of love. It can also evoke a sense of intensity or aggression. That's how we got the phrase "seeing red." Science has shown some people actually really do see the color red when they're upset—which might be linked to our ancestors' tendency as hunter-gatherers to link red with potential danger.

CODED

Here's what science says about how the colors we see can impact how we feel and act.

SECURE

Being "blue" doesn't always mean being sad. This color can be associated with stability, which is why businesses often use this color in logos or advertisements. Blue can also make us feel a sense of serenity—maybe because it reminds some people of the ocean—and blue walls have been shown to improve people's ability to study and be more productive.

CALM

Some say pink instills a sense of optimism. (Ever heard of rose-colored glasses?) Research shows, at least in small doses, pink can make us feel calmer. Too much time around pink, though, and some people grow agitated.

GLITZY
GLITTER

It's a **sparkling party decoration,** a shimmering makeup ingredient, and a dazzling addition to any craft. But there's more than meets the eye with these **tiny bits of sparkling material.**

PREHISTORIC SPARKLES

Glitter's been around since the Stone Age. Ancient Maya used chipped bits of mica, a shiny mineral, in their paintings to make them shimmer in the sun. And sometimes, what glitters really is gold—fool's gold, anyway. Pyrite, the mineral commonly called fool's gold, has been used in the past to bring a sparkle to Paleolithic cave paintings.

Glitter made an appearance in ancient forms of makeup, too. The ancient Egyptians used glitter in eyeliner. The glitter came from green malachite (a coppery iridescent mineral), galena, and even crushed-up scarab beetles.

In the 19th century, glitter was made from a much more dangerous source: glass. Now often made from shiny, colorful foil, the glitter we know today was an accidental invention in 1934.

GOING BATTY

Unicorns might not poop glitter—but bats do! Some bat species eat more than two-thirds their body weight in bugs every day, chewing up the protein-rich food source before swallowing it. The exoskeletons of these bugs are shiny and hard to digest, so the chewed-up bits, um, pass through the bat's body. The result? Shimmering nuggets of guano—bat poop.

Scientists use the glittering guano to learn more about these animals. By collecting and studying the droppings, they're able to learn more about bat diets. For instance, researchers have discovered some bats play an important role in pest control, because they eat the kinds of insects that damage crops. That means bats are saving farmers big bucks.

PRACTICAL MAGIC

What does the military have to do with glitter? Turns out, glitter has helped planes in combat do disappearing acts. Both the United States and the United Kingdom have used glitter to throw off enemy radar. Their planes released glittery strips of metal as they flew. Radar picked up on all the metal in the air, making it impossible for the enemies to pick out a plane's location.

Glitter even has crime-solving capabilities. Every manufacturer uses its own recipe for their batches of bling, giving their product its own sort of unique fingerprint. The shape, thickness, and refraction vary—and unlike other types of evidence, glitter doesn't easily degrade. Forensic scientists are able to track the thousands of different variations in a computer database—so when glitter turns up at a crime scene, investigators can match the evidence to any traces of glitter stuck to a suspected criminal. Now that's glitter for good.

YOU CAN DECORATE YOUR FOOD WITH EDIBLE GLITTER.

ECO-FRIENDLY GLITTER

Glitter is great fun—but it's also bad for the environment. The little shiny bits are hard to clean up, especially if they make their way into our water supply and out to the ocean, where marine animals can mistake it for prey. What's worse, every piece of glitter can take 400 years to decompose. Luckily there's a solution: eco-friendly glitter. The biodegradable bits are made from sustainable materials that won't harm wildlife.

Mica

CLEOPATRA AND OTHER ANCIENT EGYPTIANS WORE GLITTER MADE FROM BUGS.

NATURAL
VS. ▶
SYNTHETIC

◀ **NATURAL**
Natural gemstones form in the ground, then get mined from Earth's crust. Depending on the kind of gem, it might take millions of years to form.

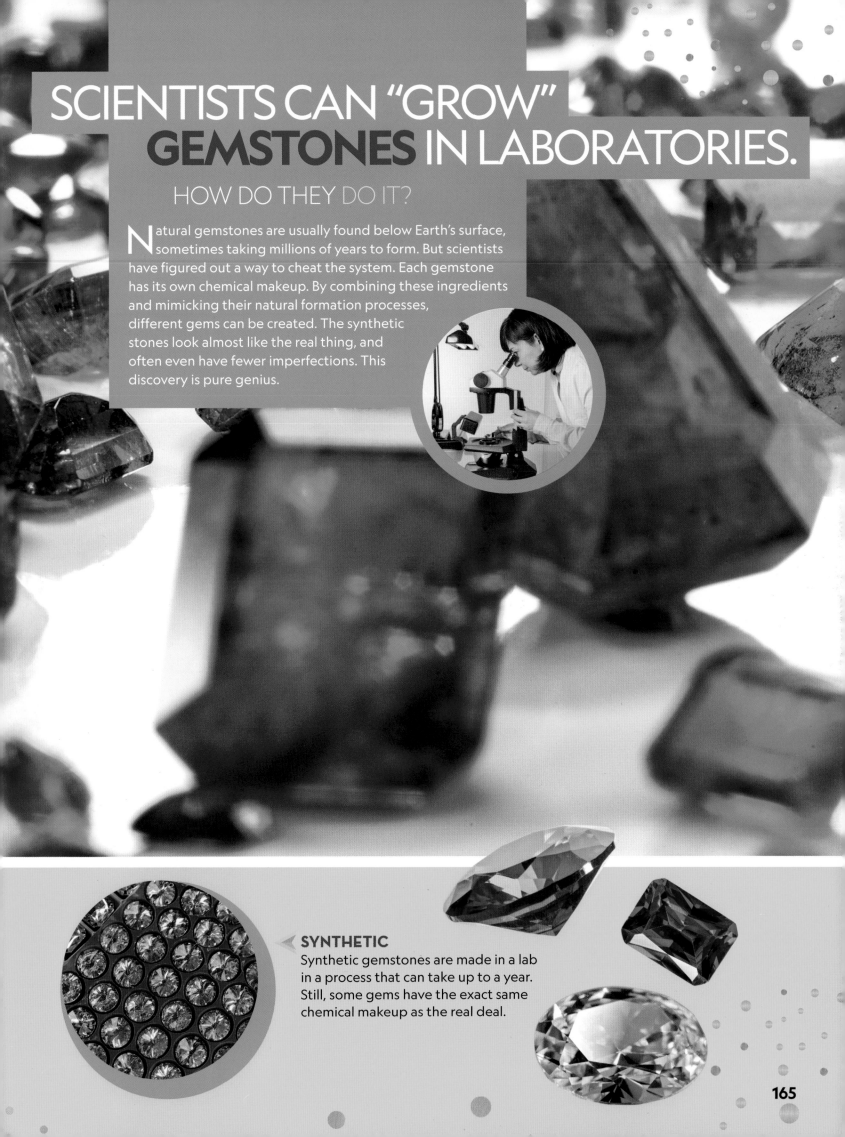

SCIENTISTS CAN "GROW" GEMSTONES IN LABORATORIES.

HOW DO THEY DO IT?

Natural gemstones are usually found below Earth's surface, sometimes taking millions of years to form. But scientists have figured out a way to cheat the system. Each gemstone has its own chemical makeup. By combining these ingredients and mimicking their natural formation processes, different gems can be created. The synthetic stones look almost like the real thing, and often even have fewer imperfections. This discovery is pure genius.

SYNTHETIC
Synthetic gemstones are made in a lab in a process that can take up to a year. Still, some gems have the exact same chemical makeup as the real deal.

LAVISH
LIGHTS

Twinkling stars and awesome auroras—oh my! Nature is filled with incredible light shows—and not just in the sky. Down on Earth, glowing creatures and glimmering volcanoes are just a few of the things to illuminate our landscape. There's never a dull moment here.

More Cool
Celestial
EVENTS

◄ **SUPERMOON**

A full moon that looks bigger and brighter because it's orbiting closer to Earth.

THE SUN LOOKS LIKE A **GIANT DIAMOND RING** DURING A TOTAL SOLAR ECLIPSE.

WHAT CAUSES THE STELLAR ACCESSORY?

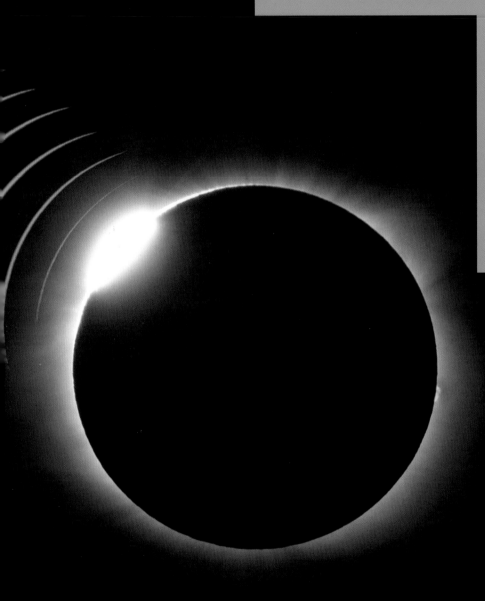

During a total solar eclipse, the moon passes between the sun and Earth, totally blocking sunlight from reaching Earth. But the moon's not totally round—it has mountains and craters that give it jagged edges. As the moon gets close to blocking the sun, sunlight passes through the moon's craters, causing lights to flash—so it looks like a giant diamond ring sparkling in the sky. The flashy lights were dubbed Baily's beads after British astronomer Francis Baily, who first observed the phenomenon in 1836.

LUNAR ECLIPSE
An event in which Earth blocks some or all of the sun's direct light from reaching a full moon.

METEOR SHOWER
Bits of comets that enter Earth's atmosphere at very high speeds, creating streaks of light as they burn up.

COMET FLYBY
An event in which a comet closely approaches and zooms past Earth.

7 Flashy FACTS About ...
BIOLUMINESCENT BLING

These flashy animals use their power to produce light—called bioluminescence—for everything from attracting mates to warding off predators.

1
Every **FIREFLY** species **FLASHES ITS LIGHT** to a different internal **RHYTHM.**

2
Bacteria inside the **HAWAIIAN BOBTAIL SQUID** work with the animal to produce **LIGHT THAT MIMICS MOONLIGHT.**

3
At night, the Maldives' **SEA OF STARS GLOWS** with **BIOLUMINESCENT PLANKTON.**

The RADIOACTIVE-LIKE GLOW from certain **MUSHROOMS** is thought to **ATTRACT INSECTS,** which spread the fungus's spores.

4

5

Some **MILLIPEDES GLOW** to scare away hungry animals—but if that doesn't work, their bodies can create **CYANIDE** to **POISON** their **PREDATORS.**

6 **CRYSTAL JELLIES,** sea creatures with clear bodies, emit **A GREEN LIGHT** from their bell when disturbed.

7

A Dutch design team hopes to one day **LIGHT STREETS WITH TREES** by adding light-producing compounds from **LIVING ORGANISMS** to their leaves.

Awesome AURORAS

The phenomenon known as an aurora adds stunning streamers of light across a starry sky. The surreal scene may happen at night, but the show originates from the brightest of places—our sun. Uncover the mystery of how these awesome light shows work.

BEST VIEWING SPOTS:
Near the North Pole (aurora borealis) and South Pole (aurora australis)

AURORA'S ALTITUDE:
60 to 600 miles (97 to 966 km) above land

EARTH'S DISTANCE FROM THE SUN:
93 million miles (150 million km)

1
The sun discharges particles that are hurtled toward Earth through solar wind.

2
Particles drawn to Earth's magnetic poles pass through the planet's magnetic shield.

3

When the particles from the sun collide with Earth's atmosphere, they meet atoms and create lights.

Nitrogen atoms emit light that's orange, red, violet, or blue.

Oxygen atoms emit green and yellow light.

THE PARTICLES FROM THE SUN TAKE 40 HOURS TO TRAVEL THROUGH SPACE TO REACH EARTH.

4

The shape of an aurora depends on how the particles enter the atmosphere.

SOME ANCIENT PEOPLE THOUGHT AURORAS WERE SOULS ON THEIR WAY TO THE AFTERLIFE OR REFLECTIONS OF WHALES SWIMMING ACROSS THE SEA.

AURORAS ARE VISIBLE FROM SPACE.

AURORAS ALSO HAVE BEEN OBSERVED ON JUPITER, SATURN, URANUS, AND NEPTUNE.

COOL CONSTELLATIONS

Connect the dots in the night sky and you'll see the stars align into stellar shapes. Behind these cosmic clusters are enchanting stories from Greek mythology.

CASSIOPEIA

Named for a vain Ethiopian queen, Cassiopeia bragged she and her daughter were more beautiful than the sea nymphs. Angered by the claim, Poseidon banished her—along with her throne—to the sky. The "W" pattern represents the five brightest stars in the constellation.

GREATER DOG

Canis Major, Latin for "greater dog," is one of Orion's hunting dogs. The canine constellation includes a seriously cool feature: Sirius A—the brightest star in the night sky.

ORION ▷▷▷▷

According to mythology, Orion was a hunter armed with an unbreakable club of solid bronze. Legend has it Orion was sent away to the sky for angering goddess Artemis. In the constellation, a cluster of seven main stars forms Orion and includes a stellar fashion accessory: the three stars that make up his belt.

BIG BEAR ▶▶▶▶

Probably one of the most popular constellations in the night sky is the Big Dipper. The formation is actually part of a much larger constellation, though: Ursa Major, or Great Bear. If you find the dipper, you'll see the dipper's cup is also the back part of the bear, with the bear's tail acting as the handle.

◀◀◀ SWAN

Phaethon, the mortal son of Helios, fell from his father's Sun Chariot into a river below. Wanting to save his friend's life, Cygnus desperately dove into the river in search of him. Observing this act of love and friendship, the gods turned Cygnus into a swan that would live forever in the sky.

NORTHERN ▶▶▶▶ CROWN

King Theseus supposedly slew a ferocious Minotaur for his beloved fiancé, Princess Ariadne. The seven stars that make up the crown represent those that were sacrificed to the Minotaur before it met its demise. After the princess died, the crown took to the sky.

HARP ▲

Apollo was said to have invented the lyre, or harp, and gifted it to Orpheus, a god whose music could tame wild animals. After Orpheus's death, Zeus placed his harp in the sky to honor the talented musician.

HYDRA ▶▶▶▶

Hercules repeatedly battled Hydra, a multiheaded monster, but each time he cut off one head, two more grew back. He managed to get rid of all but one head, but to his disappointment, he discovered the last one was immortal. Hercules wasn't deterred, though, and he buried the head under a rock, defeating the menacing monster.

BLUE
VOLCANO

The night is pitch-black. But the dark slopes of a hill inside the **crater of Kawah Ijen volcano** in Indonesia, a country in Southeast Asia, are lit up like a holiday light show. Oozing from the volcano are what look like **glowing blue rivers of lava**—but are really rivers of glowing sulfur.

An explorer watches the blue fire of Kawah Ijen.

BURNING BLUE

Glowing red lava flowing from an erupting volcano isn't unusual. Glowing sulfur is. Hot, sulfur-rich gases escape constantly from cracks called fumaroles in Kawah Ijen's crater. The gases cool when they hit the air. Some condense into liquid sulfur, which flows down the hillside. When the sulfur and leftover gases ignite, they burn bright blue and light up the night sky.

Scientists were told that sulfur miners on the volcano sometimes use torches to ignite the sulfur. The blue flames make Kawah Ijen popular with tourists, who watch from a safe distance. Recently scientists confirmed that some of the sulfur and gases also burn naturally, igniting as hot gases combine with oxygen in the air.

VOLCANO MINERS

Sulfur is a common volcanic gas, and its chemical properties are used to manufacture many things, such as rubber. But it's so plentiful in Kawah Ijen's crater that miners make a dangerous daily trek into the crater to collect sulfur from a fumarole near an acid lake.

"The local people pipe the gases from the fumarole through ceramic pipes," says John Pallister, a geologist with the Cascades Volcano Observatory in Washington State, U.S.A. He has walked into the crater himself, wearing a gas mask for protection against the clouds of acid that rise from the lake. "They spray the pipes with water from a spring," he says. This cools the gases and causes them to condense into molten sulfur. The sulfur then cools and hardens into rock.

Using this method, miners get more usable rock faster than if they just collected scattered pieces. They smash up the rock with metal bars, stuff the pieces into baskets, and carry them out of the crater on their backs. The loads are heavy—between 100 and 200 pounds (45 and 91 kg) apiece.

READING THE DANGER ZONE

Miners face another danger: a huge eruption. Kawah Ijen's last big eruption was almost 200 years ago, but the volcano is still active. A big eruption could endanger hundreds of miners and tourists.

Indonesian scientists want to find a way to predict a big eruption in time to keep everyone safe. But the deep acid lake makes it difficult to pick up the usual signals that warn of a coming volcanic eruption. For example, certain gases are usually more abundant right before an eruption. But in this lake, those gases dissolve in the deep water before they can register on geologists' monitoring equipment.

As scientists search for ways to predict this unusual volcano's behavior, Kawah Ijen's blue fires continue to attract audiences who appreciate the volcano's amazing glow.

INDONESIA IS A GROUP OF MORE THAN 17,500 ISLANDS OFF THE COAST OF SOUTHEAST ASIA. IT IS THE LARGEST COUNTRY IN THE REGION.

Sulfur lake of Kawah Ijen

Workers carry sulfur mined from Kawah Ijen.

WHEN THE VOLCANO ON THE TINY INDONESIAN ISLAND OF KRAKATAU ERUPTED IN AUGUST 1883, IT COULD BE HEARD THOUSANDS OF MILES AWAY.

More WEIRD WATERS ➤

➤ **LAKE NATRON**
Tanzania
The surface's salty crust gets its hue from microorganisms in the water.

LIGHTNING STRIKES VENEZUELA'S LAKE MARACAIBO ROUGHLY 1.2 MILLION TIMES A YEAR.

SO LIGHTNING REALLY DOES STRIKE THE SAME PLACE TWICE?

Yes, and then some! This spot actually gets more lightning than anywhere else in the world, sometimes seeing thousands of strikes in the span of a single hour. Experts aren't sure why the lake seems to be a hotbed for the electrifying activity, but some guess it has more to do with the air above the lake than the lake itself.

Locals call it "Catatumbo lightning" after the name of the river that enters into the lake. They take such pride in the phenomenon that lightning bolts are incorporated into one Venezuelan state's flag.

JELLYFISH LAKE
Palau
Millions of golden jellyfish follow the sun as they swim in this lake in Southeast Asia.

CAÑO CRISTALES
Colombia
Sun causes colorful aquatic plants to blossom on the bottom of this river.

BOILING LAKE
Dominica
Around its edges, water here reaches a roaring 197°F (92°C).

ECHIDNA
Where: Australia, Indonesia, and Papua New Guinea

With a spine-covered body like a porcupine, a long-beaked echidna might not look like something you'd want to eat. But in their native range, these mammals are often hunted for food. When it comes to catching their own food, long-beaked echidnas utilize their tongues—covered in yet more spines—to help them capture worms and other insects.

PLATYPUS >
Where: Australia

This duck-billed critter faces a threat with an equally interesting name: yabby traps. Meant to catch crayfish and crabs, these nets accidentally snare hungry platypuses, too. Raising awareness about the dangerous traps is helping to stop their use.

ARK of

SUMATRAN TIGER
Where: Indonesia

Isolated on the island of Sumatra in Indonesia, this tiger subspecies is threatened by poaching and habitat loss. Though considered a "big cat," this feline's not nearly as big as its tiger relatives, reaching just half the size of its Siberian counterpart. Scientists think the cat may have developed as a smaller species due to the limited space on its island habitat.

GREATER BILBY

Where: Australia

The bilby—also known as the bandicoot—is preyed on by an unexpected killer: feral cats. The felines, paired with invasive foxes, have caused this adorable bunny-like creature to dwindle in numbers. Solitary and nocturnal, the bilby hides out in underground burrows during the day to stay safe.

PANGOLIN

Where: Africa and Asia

Covered in tough scales, the pangolin looks kind of like a living, breathing artichoke. These scales, which poachers often hunt and kill the animals to get, are made of the same substance found in your fingernails. Poachers sell the scales for use in Chinese medicine, though the scales haven't been scientifically proven to have healing powers.

LIGHT

To draw attention to threatened or endangered species, Australia's Taronga Zoo lit up its grounds with lanterns of larger-than-life creatures.

ASIAN ELEPHANT

Where: Southeast Asia

Elephants in both Africa and Asia face habitat loss and are prized by poachers for their ivory tusks, used to make souvenir carvings and other goods. What makes an Asian elephant's tusks even more rare? All African elephants have tusks, but only some male Asian elephants have them.

PYGMY TARSIER

Where: Indonesia

One of the world's most endangered primates, the pygmy tarsier was once thought to be extinct. The nocturnal creature, which relies on the forest canopy to block moonlight from exposing it to predators, is well known for its giant eyes. Each of the tarsier's eyes is about the same size as its brain.

Fluorescent
FUN

By ABSORBING SURROUNDING LIGHT, these fascinating things GLOW IN THE DARK.

SHEEP OF THE SEA
When this sea slug was discovered in 2015, it made people around the world go "aww!" A banker on vacation captured images of the never-before-seen creature—later dubbed the "leaf sheep"—while scuba diving off the coast of Bali, in Indonesia. Like plants, these critters can take sunlight and turn it into energy.

FREAKY ICE CREAM

This frozen treat will really light you up. Made with fluorescent proteins found in jellyfish, the glowing ice cream interacts with the pH on your tongue. The more it's licked, the brighter it glows. But it'll cost you—one scoop goes for $225.

GEM JUSTICE

Lots of gems sparkle in the light—but not many shine when the lights are out. Held up to an ultraviolet light, certain gems can emit their own glow, including the famed Hope Diamond. When researchers studied the glow of the rare stone and compared it to other glowing gems, they discovered something that surprised them: Each gem glowed a different shade and for a different length of time, meaning each had its own unique "fingerprint." With this information, it could be easier to track stolen jewels or identify fakes.

GOBLIN'S GOLD

Just like a true goblin, you won't see this special species of moss out and about aboveground. Commonly called goblin's gold, the glowing moss is adapted to growing in dark places with limited light, like inside caves or animal burrows, where most other plants can't survive.

RIBBETING FIND

You'd think having a name like the "polka-dot tree frog" would be enough fun for one amphibian—but not so. In normal light, this frog's body is a muted yellow-green with red spots. But under ultraviolet light, the animal's body shines in a neon blue-green. Scientists think the frog might use its glowing powers to communicate with other frogs, especially to signal its location to attract a mate.

OMEGA CENTAURI, OUR GALAXY'S BIGGEST AND BRIGHTEST STAR CLUSTER, GLITTERS WITH 10 MILLION COLORFUL STARS.

WHAT'S GOING ON IN THIS SPARKLY SHOT?

This famous photograph shows about 100,000 of the sparkly stars. NASA's Hubble telescope captured the image, showing a cluster of stars 16,000 light-years from Earth. The photo captures stars, which can "live" for a trillion years, in different stages of their life cycle. The yellow-white stars are adults. Toward the end of their normal lives, these stars become cooler and larger, turning to orange dots. As the stars continue to cool and expand, they become red giants.

Stars are basically big balls of gas—mostly helium and hydrogen. The bright red stars will swell to be several times larger than the sun, then start to shed their gases and sparkle a brilliant blue. When the gases run out, the stars reach the end of their lives, becoming faint blue dots called white dwarfs. Other stars in the snapshot are "blue stragglers": older stars that got a new lease on life by colliding and merging with other stars.

More STELLAR STARS

HE 2359-2844 AND HE 1256-2738 These heavy metal subdwarfs are covered with 10,000 times more lead than the sun.

PSR J1719-1438B
Thanks to another star, this former star became a giant diamond planet five times bigger than Earth.

OH 231.8+04.2
Formed when a star died, the Rotten Egg Nebula contains sulfur that, combined with other elements, gives off a bad stench.

HD 140283
Scientists estimate the oldest known star in the galaxy, the Methuselah star, is 14.46 billion years old—give or take 800 million years.

INDEX

INDEX

INDEX

CREDITS

Abbreviations: AL = Alamy; GI = Getty Images; MP = Minden Pictures; NGIC = National Geographic Image Collection; SS = Shutterstock

COVER, (red marquis shaped gem), Universal Images Group North America LLC/DeAgostini/AL; (orange topaz gem), The Natural History Museum/AL; (blue sapphire gem), Edwardkaraa/Dreamstime; (diamond), Doug Armand/GI; (palace) Art Konovalov/SS; (green peridot gem), Richard Leeney/Dorling Kindersley/GI; (Imperial Crown of Russia), Album/Fine Art Images/Newscom; (Tutankhamun's funeral mask), robertharding/AL Stock Photo; (full suit of armor), mg7/iStockphoto; (gold coins), David Spencer/Palm Beach Post/ZUMA Pres/AL Stock Photo; (hummingbird in flight), Michael and Patricia Fogden/MP; (Elvis's ring with pink stone), Tom Donoghue/Polaris/Newscom; (rectangular diamond), Brand X; (blue aquamarine gem), Richard Leeney/Dorling Kindersley/GI; (blue morpho butterfly), Robert S. Oakes/NGIC; (diamonds picture borders), Mishatc/DS; (silver shiny background in letters), rangizzz/SS; back cover (green pear-shaped gem), Richard Leeney/Dorling Kindersley/GI; (purple Tanzanite gems), Science Photo Library/GI; (St. Edward's Crown), Jack Hill/AFP/GI; (horse in suit of armor), Fletcher Fund, 1921/ Metropolitan Museum of Art; (astronaut golden helmet), Claude Thibault/AL Stock Photo; (red Rhodochrosite gems), Universal Images Group North America LLC/DeAgostini/AL; (orange Topaz gem), The Natural History Museum/AL; spine (hummingbird sitting), Glenn Bartley/All Canada Photos/GI; (blue sapphire gem), Edwardkaraa/ DS; (red Rhodochrosite gems), Universal Images Group North America LLC/DeAgostini/AL; (green emerald crystals), Kirill Makarov/SS; (blue aquamarine gem), Richard Leeney/Dorling Kindersley/GI; **FRONT MATTER:** 1, Jack Hill/AFP/GI; 2 (UP LE), M. Watson/ardea.com; 2 (emerald ring), photo-world/SS; 2-3 (aquamarine), PjrStudio/AL; 2 (UP RT), Cody Duncan/age fotostock; 2 (LO), Metropolitan Museum of Art; 3 (rectangular diamond), Brand X Pictures/GI; 3 (UP), Milous Chab/DS.com; 3 (skateboard), Matthew Willet; 4 (UP), Album/Fine Art Images/Newscom; 4 (CTR), AL; 4 (LO), Smit/SS; 5 (bear), Krys Bailey/AL; 5 (lightning), Gail Johnson/GI; 5 (purple gem), Patrick Llewelyn-Davies/Science Source; 5 (LO), J. Palys/SS; 6 (UP), Thornton Cohen/AL; 6 (RT), Georgette Douwma/MP; 6 (LO), SS; 7 (RT), Harris Brisbane Dick Fund, 1939/The Metropolitan Museum; 7 (LE), Olivia Mon/SS; **CHAPTER 1:** 8 (garnet stone), PjrStudio/AL; 8-9 (big diamond), Doug Armand/GI; 8-9 (turquoise), Antony Souter/AL; 8 (amethyst gem), Greg C Grace/AL; 8 (pearl), Visage/GI; 8 (blue sapphire), Edward Karaa/DS.com; 8 (round ruby), Fuse/GI; 8 (amethyst geode), RF Company/AL; 8 (rectangular diamond), Brand X Pictures/GI; 8 (opal), Peter Harholdt/ SuperStock; 9 (stack of rings), kyoshino/GI; 9 (aquamarine), PjrStudio/AL; 9 (diamond rocks), Eric Nathan/AL; 9 (aquamarine gem), Richard Leeney/GI; 9 (peridot gem), Richard Leeney/GI; 9 (garnet geode), Gemstone/AL; 9 (garnet stone), PjrStudio/AL; 9 (blue sapphire), Edward Karaa/DS.com; 9 (aquamarine gem), Richard Leeney/GI; 9 (quartz), Nastya22/SS; 10 (opal), Peter Harholdt/SuperStock; 10 (topaz), The Natural History Museum/AL; 10 (LE), PjrStudio/AL; 10 (amethyst gem), Greg C Grace/AL; 10 (aquamarine gem), Richard Leeney/GI; 10 (LO RT), PjrStudio/ AL; 10 (amethyst ring), Dimas Barrantes/AL; 10 (pearl), Visage/GI; 10 (round ruby), Fuse/GI; 11 (diamond rocks), Eric Nathan/AL; 11 (UP RT), Doug Armand/GI; 11 (emerald ring), photo-world/SS; 11 (LE), Greg C Grace/AL; 11 (emerald rock), Jan Sochor/AL; 11 (pearl necklace), sviridov/SS; 11 (LO RT), The Natural History Museum/AL; 12 (ruby gem), Joao Virissimo/DS; 12 (UP RT), Tarzhanova/SS; 12 (LO LE), Richard Leeney/GI; 12 (blue sapphire), Edward Karaa/DS. com; 12 (LO RT), Walter Geiersperger/GI; 13 (UP LE), Peter Harholdt/SuperStock; 13 (opal rock), Gary Ombler/Dorling Kindersley/Science Source; 13 (turquoise bracelet), AR Images/AL; 13 (LO RT), Phil Degginger/Jack Clark Collection/ AL; 13 (LO LE), Shawn Hempel/AL; 13 (UP RT), Wilawan Khasawong/AL; 14-15 (BACKGROUND), Cagla Acikgoz/SS; 14 (CTR), josefkubes/SS; 14 (LO CTR), Ulrich Baumgarten/GI; 14 (LO RT), vvoe/SS; 15 (LO LE), Albert Russ/SS; 15 (gold nuggets), Eli Maier/SS; 15 (pyrite crystals), Daniel127001/DS; 16-17, Millard H. Sharp/Science Source; 18 (RT), De Agostini Picture Library/UIG/Newscom; 18 (LO), PA Images/AL; 19 (UP LE), Steve Hamblin/AL; 19 (CTR RT), TopFoto/ The Image Works; 19 (LO LE), Album/Fine Art Images/Newscom; 20-21 (BACKGROUND), NguyenQuocThang/SS; 20 (CTR), Photo12/UIG/GI; 20 (fluorite), Mark A. Schneider/Science Source; 20 (toothbrush), oksana2010/SS; 20 (feldspar), Fokin Oleg/SS; 20 (jug), Hintau Aliaksei/SS; 21 (corundum), Gozzoli/SS; 21 (watch), National Geographic Society; 21 (gypsum), michal812/SS; 21 (Twinkie), Michael Neelon(misc)/AL; 22 (UP LE), Universal Images Group North America LLC/DeAgostini/AL; 22 (UP RT), Photographer/AL Stock Photo; 22 (LO LE), Albert Russ/SS; 22 (LO RT), Universal Images Group North America LLC/DeAgostini/AL; 23 (UP RT), Albert Russ/SS; 23 (tanzanite), The Natural History Museum/AL; 23 (UP LE), Charles D. Winters/Science Source; 23 (LO LE), Millard H. Sharp/Science Source; 23 (LO RT), Matteo Chinellato/Photoshot/Newscom; 24 (BACKGROUND), miljko/GI; 24, J. Palys/SS; 24 (CTR), Byjeng/SS; 25 (UP RT), SS; 25 (LO RT), Boltin Picture Library/Bridgeman Images; 25 (LO LE), The Natural History Museum/AL; 26 (scepter), GraphicaArtis/GI; 26 (quarry), POSNER/SS; 26 (pink diamonds), Lauren Campbell/Caters News Agency; 26 (colored diamonds), Peter Macdiarmid/GI; 26 (diamond cluster), Phillip Hayson/GI; 26 (circular diamond), Mishatc/ DS.com; 26 (rectangular diamond), Brand X Pictures/GI; 26 (rectangular diamond), Brand X Pictures/GI; 27 (UP RT), PHAS/UIG/GI; 27 (large diamond), ODM/SS; 27 (volcano), Photographerlondon/DS.com; 27 (LO LE), Private Collection/The Stapleton Collection/Bridgeman Images; 27 (rectangular diamond), Brand X Pictures/GI; 27 (rectangular diamond), Brand X Pictures/GI; 27 (circular diamond), Mishatc/DS.com; **CHAPTER 2:** 28-29, Carrie Vonderhaar/Ocean Futures Society/NGIC; 30-31 (BACKGROUND), Hintau Aliaksei/SS; 30 (LO CTR), Rudi Sebastian/GI; 30 (LO RT), Robert Valentic/MP; 31 (LO LE), Staffan Widstrand/Nature Picture Library; 31 (CTR), David Fleetham/ Nature Picture Library; 31 (LO RT), Jak Wonderly; 32, All Canada Photos/AL; 33 (UP), Robert Whyte; 33 (CTR), K. Nakao/SS; 33 (LO LE), NHPA/Photoshot; 33 (LO RT), Mathisa/SS; 34 (UP LE), asharkyu/SS; 34 (UP RT), John Cancalosi/ AL; 34 (LO), Thomas Marent/MP/GI; 35 (UP RT), Chelsea Cameron/SS; 35 (UP LE), Matt Propert/National Geographic Society; 35 (LO LE), Michael D. Kern/MP; 35 (LO RT), Tammy Wolfe/AL; 36 (LE), Tier Und Naturfotografie J und C Sohns/GI; 36 (RT), Splash News/Newscom; 36 (UP), juefraphoto/GI; 37 (RT), imageBROKER/AL; 37 (CTR), Amanda Edwards/WireImage/GI; 37 (LO CTR), dpa picture alliance/AL; 37 (LO), ROPI/ZUMAPRESS/Newscom; 37 (UP), y-mages/ GI; 37 (LE), JPagetRFphotos/AL; 38-39 (BACKGROUND), Sascha Burkard/SS; 38 (LO CTR), Michael and Patricia Fogden/MP/NGIC; 38 (LO RT), SuperStock/age fotostock; 39 (cuttlefish), Ethan Daniels/SS; 39 (husky), ANGHI/SS; 39 (mantis shrimp), Sean Chinn/greatwhitesean/AL; 39 (chameleon), Sebastian Duda/SS; 40 (LE), Donald M. Jones/MP; 40 (RT), Rod Williams/MP; 41 (UP LE), Bill Gozansky/AL; 41 (UP RT), Tim Laman/NGIC; 41 (CTR LE), Thomas Marent/MP; 41 (LO RT), Paul D Stewart/MP; 42-43 (BACKGROUND), VW Pics/GI; 43 (LO), Herman Wong HM/SS; 43 (UP CTR), H. Bellmann/picture alliance/blickwinkel/H/Newscom; 43 (UP), Agarianna76/SS; 43 (UP CTR), Pérez-de la Fuente, et al., "Evolution of camouflage in insects," PNAS, Dec 2012, 109 (52) 21414-21419/Illustration by J. A. Peñas; 44 (UP LE), Oliver Bunic/Bloomberg/GI; 44 (CTR RT), Artaporn Puthikampol/SS; 44 (UP RT), Rosa Jay/SS; 44 (LO LE), alessandro_pinto/iStock/GI; 45 (UP RT), Sotheby's/SS; 45 (CTR), Taylor Weidman/Bloomberg/GI; 45 (RT), Cem Kaplan/AL; 45 (LO LE), Muellek Josef/SS; 45 (CTR LE), sevenke/SS; 45 (bee), lightpoet/SS; 45 (bee), lightpoet/SS; 46, Maxim Tupikov/SS; 47 (UP RT), Joel Sartore/NGIC; 47 (CTR RT), Paulo Whitaker/Reuters; 47 (LO LE), WaterFrame/AL; **CHAPTER 3:** 48 (LO RT), Gabbro/AL; 48 (LE), Kenneth Garrett/NGIC; 48 (CTR), Bates Littlehales/NGIC; 48-49 (standing figures), Kenneth Garrett/NGIC; 49 (CTR), Jan Mitchell and Sons Collection, Gift of Jan Mitchell, 1991/The Metropolitan Museum; 49 (LO), akg-images/François Guénet/The Image Works; 49 (UP), Richard Barnes/NGIC; 50-51 (BACKGROUND), PhotoStock-Israel/Science Source; 50 (cochineal insects), Chris Howes/Wild Places Photography/AL; 50 (rhubarb roots), Cedar_Liu/GI; 51 (UP), Classic Image/AL; 51 (cuttlefish ink), The Natural History Museum/The Image Works; 51 (onion skins), AngelikaSh/SS; 51 (eucalyptus), Noppharat4969/SS; 51 (avocado pits), topseller/SS; 52, Fer Gregory/SS; 53 (UP RT), Look and Learn/Bridgeman Images; 53 (CTR), Peter Horree/AL; 53 (LO RT), Look and Learn/Bridgeman Images; 53 (LO LE), Charles Walker/Topfoto/The Image Works; 54 (UP LE), Manuel Litran/GI; 54 (UP RT), O. Louis Mazzatenta/NGIC; 54 (LO), age fotostock/AL; 55 (UP LE), RMN-Grand Palais/Art Resource, NY; 55 (UP RT), Gift and Bequest of Alice K. Bache, 1974, 1977/The Metropolitan Museum; 55 (LO LE), Philippe Maillard/akg-images/Newscom; 55 (LO RT), World History Archive/AL; 56, Jasmin Awad/SS; 57 (UP), Zuma Press, Inc./AL; 57 (RT), Cleveland Museum of Art, OH, USA/Purchase from the J. H. Wade Fund/Bridgeman Images; 57 (LO), Aleksandar Todorovic/SS; 58 (UP LE), Uber Bilder/AL; 58 (UP RT), Print Collector/GI; 58 (CTR LE), NASA; 58 (CTR RT), Keystone-France/GI; 58 (LO RT), Heritage Auctions, HA.com; 58 (LO LE), Underwood Archives/GI; 59 (UP RT), Moviestore collection Ltd/AL; 59 (CTR LE), Dorotheum; 59 (CTR RT), UniversalImagesGroup/GI; 59 (LO LE), Tolga Akmen/AFP/GI; 59 (LO CTR RT), Library of Congress, Prints and Photographs Collection [LC-USZ62-111797]; 59 (CTR RT), Library of Congress, Prints and Photographs Collection [LC-USZC4-11913]; 60, akg-images/Newscom; 61 (UP LE), Heritage Image Partnership Ltd/AL; 61 (UP RT), Duncan McGlynn/Splash News/Newscom; 61 (CTR LE), Universal History Archive/GI; 61 (LO RT), Paul Koudounaris/BNPS/SS; 62-63, Kenneth Garrett/NGIC; 62-63 (BACKGROUND), ilolab/SS; 64 (CTR), Francois Guillot/AFP/GI; 64 (UP), Elnur/SS; 64 (LO), Design Pics Inc/NGIC; 65 (UP RT), Matthew Fearn/PA Images/GI; 65 (LO RT), canadastock/SS; 65 (UP LE), Julian Parker/UK Press/GI; 66 (UP), Art Konovalov/SS; 66 (CTR), Songquan Deng/DS; 66 (LO), Nicholas Courtney/SS; 67 (UP), imageBROKER/SS; 67 (CTR), wassiliy-architect/ SS; 67 (LO), Helen Cathcart/Zuma Press/Newscom; **CHAPTER 4:** 68-69, Smit/SS; 70 (CTR LE), Owen Smith/AL; 70 (LO CTR), Owen Smith/AL; 70 (LO RT), chaoss/SS; 71 (UP), ChameleonsEye/SS; 71 (CTR), Johan Swanepoel/SS; 71 (LO), Mark Horton/AL; 72 (UP LE), ppart/SS; 72 (UP RT), ppart/SS; 72 (LO LE), Eye-Stock/AL; 72 (LO RT), powerofforever/GI; 73 (UP RT), Glyn Thomas/AL; 73 (CTR RT), Eye-Stock/AL; 73 (LO LE), The Banknote Book; 73 (LO RT), Glyn Thomas/AL; 74 (UP), Brian McEntire/SS; 74 (UP), Brian McEntire/SS; 74 (CTR LE), Everett - Art/SS; 74 (ice cream), Elena Elisseeva/ iStockphoto; 74 (ice cream), Elena Elisseeva/iStockphoto; 74 (stamp), Stamp Collection/AL; 74 (LO LE), Jennifer Barrow/DS; 74 (LO RT), Dan Kosmayer/SS; 74-75 (BACKGROUND), rangizzz/SS; 75 (UP LE), Editorial Image, LLC/AL; 75 (CTR LE), Mike Clarke/AFP/GI; 75 (LO RT), Smith Collection/Gado/GI; 75 (UP RT), ; 77, Detlev Van Ravenswaay/Science Source; 78 (LE), Seashell World/SS; 78 (RT), Rtsutdio/SS; 79 (UP LE), Elena Schweitzer/SS; 79 (UP RT), Madlen/SS; 79 (CTR RT), Michael Runkel/robertharding/Newscom; 79 (LO CTR LE), Aleem Zahid Khan/SS; 79 (LO LE), Aleem Zahid Khan/SS; 79 (LO RT), bigacis/SS; 80, United Fibers/Splash/Newscom; 81 (UP), Martin Bialecki/dpa/AL; 81 (LO), Karl Gehring/The Denver Post/GI; 82-83 (BACKGROUND), De Agostini/A. Dagli Orti/Granger, NYC; 82 (LO), Pictures from History/Granger, NYC; 83 (UP), Peter Horree/AL; 83 (LO LE), duncan1890/GI; 83 (LO RT), Archive Photos/GI; **CHAPTER 5:** 84-85, Gert Buter/MP; 86, xinhua Xinhua News Agency/Newscom; 87 (UP LE), imageBROKER/AL; 87 (CTR RT), Stephen Saks/GI; 87 (CTR LE), Media Drum World/AL; 87 (LO RT), Budkov Denis/SS; 88-89 (UP), Norberto Duarte/ AFP/GI; 88 (CTR), Peter Adams/GI; 89 (CTR), Cyril Ruoso/MP; 89 (LO), The Natural History Museum/AL; 90 (UP LE), suronin/SS; 90 (LO), Eranga Jayawardena/AP Photo; 90 (UP RT), David Santiago Garcia/Photoshot/Newscom; 91 (UP), Bbar/DS; 91 (RT), Tom Murphy/NGIC; 91 (LE), Joe Carini/The Image Works; 92 (UP LE), All Canada Photos/AL; 92 (UP RT), Tappasan Phurisamrit/SS; 92 (LO LE), Suthasinee K/SS; 93 (UP RT), Cornelia Doerr/GI; 93 (UP LE), AFP/GI; 93 (LO LE), Rebecca Picard/DS; 93 (LO RT), matteo_it/SS; 94-95, Jose Fuste Raga/GI; 96-97 (BACKGROUND), Vlad61/SS; 96 (brain coral), John A. Anderson/SS; 96 (tree coral), Fiona Ayerst/SS; 97 (cauliflower coral), Damsea/SS; 97 (bubblegum coral), Universal History Archive/UIG/GI; 97 (bird's nest coral), blickwinkel/AL; 98 (UP), Sergey Pesterev/GI; 98 (CTR), ARCO/Schunk, H/age fotostock; 98 (LO), robertharding/AL; 99 (UP RT), A. Rose/picture alliance/blickwinkel/Newscom; 99 (UP LE), Michael Runkel/robertharding; 99 (CTR RT), Richard Bizley/Science Source; 99 (LO LE), Simon Fraser/Science Photo Library/GI; 100, Christopher Ewing/DS; 101 (RT), Kris Wiktor/SS; 101 (LO), Inge Johnsson/age fotostock; 102-103 (BACKGROUND), CathyKeifer/iStock/GI; 102 (pitcher plants), Take Photo/SS; 102 (venus flytrap), Chris Mattison/Nature Picture Library; 103 (cobra lily), David R. Frazier/Science Source; 103 (butterwort), Claus Meyer/MP; 103 (rainbow plant), blickwinkel/AL; **CHAPTER 6:** 104-105, Michael and Patricia Fogden/MP; 106-107 (BACKGROUND), e_rik/SS; 106 (mercury), Science Photo Library/GI; 106 (thermometer), Robyn Mackenzie/DS; 106 (lead), Russell Lappa/GI; 106 (dumbbell), Timothy Geiss/SS; 107 (aluminum), Jorgeprz/DS; 107 (can), Coprid/SS; 107 (gold), Susan E. Degginger/AL; 107 (necklace), Planner/SS; 107 (platinum), Sementer/SS; 107 (rings), kritskaya/SS; 107 (copper), Zelenskaya/SS; 107 (pot), Michael Kraus/SS; 108, Ken McKay/ITV/SS; 109 (UP RT), claude thibault/AL; 109 (LE), Kateryna Kon/Science Photo Library/Newscom; 109 (RT), Poznyakov/SS; 109 (LO LE), michael norcia/Sygma/GI; 110 (LE), Richard Brown/AL; 110 (RT), mr_piboon/GI; 110 (LO), stellalevi/GI; 111 (UP LE), William Manning/AL; 111 (RT), Media Mode/SS; 111 (LE), Jay Yuan/SS; 111 (LO RT), vincent abbey/AL; 112 (LE), Bashford Dean Memorial Collection, Gift of Helen Fahnestock Hubbard, in memory of her father, Harris C. Fahnestock, 1929/The Metropolitan Museum of Art; 112 (RT), Bequest of George C. Stone, 1935/The Metropolitan Museum of Art; 112 (LO RT), Fletcher Fund, 1921/The Metropolitan Museum of Art; 112-113 (UP), Gift of William H. Riggs, 1913/The Metropolitan Museum of Art; 113 (UP RT), Bequest of George C. Stone, 1935/ The Metropolitan Museum of Art; 113 (RT), Andy Crawford/GI; 113 (LE), mg7/iStockphoto; 114, Jag_cz/SS; 115 (UP), Franck Fife/AFP/GI; 115 (RT), David Becker/NHLI via GI; 115 (Jets ring), Sporting News/GI; 115 (Broncos ring), Jason O. Watson/GI; 115 (Packers ring), Jason O. Watson/GI; 116-117 (BACKGROUND), Zhukova Valentyna/SS; 116 (CTR), Mark Ralston/AFP/GI; 116 (RT), Hiroshi Higuchi/GI; 117 (LE), Oliver Furrer/GI; 117 (RT), NASA/JPL/Caltech; 118 (LE), Oliver Lucanus/MP; 118 (RT), Glenn Bartley/GI; 119 (UP), David Shale/naturepl.com; 119 (CTR), Steve Downer/ardea.com; 119 (LO), Michael and Patricia Fogden/MP; 120 (UP), Nature Collection/AL; 120 (LO), Martin Creasser/AL; 121 (UP), Alex Mustard/naturepl.com; 121 (CTR), John Abbott/naturepl.com; 121 (LO), Michael and Patricia Fogden/MP; 122-123 (UP LE), Alex Ferro/Jogos Rio 2016/Handout/GI; 123 (LO), Milos Bicanski/GI; 123 (UP), Alex Ferro/Jogos Rio 2016/ Handout/GI; **CHAPTER 7:** 124-125, Joshua Sweeney; 126-127 (BACKGROUND), Anton Rogozin/SS; 126 (CTR), Tappasan Phurisamrit; 126 (RT), vm/GI; 127 (LE), vixit/SS; 127 (CTR), Michael Flippo/DS; 127 (RT), CSP_imstocks/age fotostock; 128 (LE), Conrad Maldives Rangali Island/Cover Images/Newscom; 128 (RT), robertharding/AL; 129 (UP), Pan Yulong/ Xinhua/AL; 129 (LE), Ray Evans/AL; 129 (RT), Henrik Lindvall/AL; 129 (CTR LE), Giovanni De Sandre/ZUMAPRESS/ Newscom; 130 (CTR RT), Songquan Deng/SS; 130 (LO LE), Matthew Willet; 130 (LO RT), Matthew Willet; 131 (UP), Cobalt Aircraft; 131 (RT), 2017 Golden Eagle Luxury Trains; 131 (LE), Solent News/Splash News/Newscom; 131 (LO), Michael Cole/GI; 132 (UP LE), pixelfit/GI; 132 (UP RT), Bon Appetit/AL; 132 (LO), Fotosearch/agefotostock; 133 (UP RT), The Asahi Shimbun/GI; 133 (UP LE), Katsumi Kasahara/AP Photo; 133 (LO LE), Bob Gibbons/MP; 133 (LO RT), Fresnel/SS; 134, MGM/Kobal/SS; 135 (UP), GI; 135 (RT), Splash News/AL; 135 (LE), Lucasfilm/Fox/Kobal/SS; 136, CB2/ZOB/ Newscom; 137 (UP LE), VeryFirstTo.com/SS; 137 (UP RT), wanderworldimages/AL; 137 (CTR LE), dleiva/AL; 137 (LO RT), Martin Thomas Photography/AL; 138-139, Krys Bailey/AL; 140 (LE), Tatiana Belova/DS; 140 (RT), Intellistudies/SS; 141 (RT), mohamed alwerdany/SS; 141 (LO), CP DC Press/SS; 142 (UP), HUGHES HervÂ/GI; 142 (LO), David Henley/ Pictures From Asia/Newscom; 143 (UP), Diego Grandi/AL; 143 (LO), Burak Akbulut/Anadolu Agency; **CHAPTER 8:** 144-145, Stocktrek Images, Inc./AL; 146-147 (BACKGROUND), Solvin Zankl/MP; 146 (CTR), thefontbandit/SS; 146 (RT), Paul Kay/NHPA/Photoshot/Newscom; 147 (LE), David Littschwager/NGIC; 147 (CTR), Image Courtesy of Dr. Dimitri Deheyn, Scripps Institution of Oceanography, UC San Diego; 147 (RT), Jak Wonderly/National Geographic; 148, Watcharin S/SS; 149 (UP), ANCH/SS; 149 (LE), Brendan Smialowski/AFP/GI; 149 (RT), Titima Ongkantong/SS; 149 (LO), Carolyn Franks/SS; 150-151 (BACKGROUND), Blackout Concepts/AL; 151 (RT), Herald Hugo/AP Photo; 152 (UP), George Grall/NGIC; 152 (LE), Cathy Keifer/SS; 153 (UP), Reinhard Dirscherl/GI; 153 (LO), WaterFrame/AL; 154 (UP), moosehenderson/SS; 154 (LO), JodiJacobson/GI; 155 (UP), Subaqueosshutterbug/iStockphoto; 155 (RT), Suwat Sirivutcharungchit/SS; 155 (LE), mikroman6/GI; 156 (LE), The Natural History Museum/AL; 156 (RT), Christies/ Bournemouth News/SS; 156 (LO), Leela Mei/SS; 156-157 (UP), Sebastian Janicki/SS; 156-157 (BACKGROUND), rangizzz/ SS; 157 (UP), NASA/JPL-Caltech; 157 (LE), David Aguilar/National Geographic Society; 157 (CTR RT), Phillip Hayson/GI; 157 (RT), T. Rector/NOAO/AURA/NSF/Hubble Heritage Team/STScI/NASA/Science Source; 157 (LO), Victor Habbick Visions/Science Source; 158-159 (BACKGROUND), Volodymyr Tverdokhlib/SS; 158 (CTR), Chat9780/DS.com; 158 (RT), Lazyllama/DS.com; 159 (CTR), Efired/SS; 159 (Chicago Bean), Kelly vanDellen/SS; 159 (beans), Kasinv/DS.com; 159 (marbles), AntiMartina/GI; 159 (rocks), jean schweitzer/SS; 160 (LE), Buffy1982/SS; 160 (RT), Dean Pennala/ Shutterstock; 160 (LO), Sari Oneal/SS; 161 (UP RT), Image Source/GI; 161 (UP LE), Brand X Pictures; 161 (LO LE), Adrian Kaye/SS; 161 (LO RT), CHEN HSI FU/SS; 162, Leigh Prather/SS; 163 (UP), Julie Thurston/GI; 163 (LO), PjrStudio/ AL; 164-165 (BACKGROUND), murboy/GI; 164 (CTR), Corbin17/AL; 164 (diamond), ©Doug Armand/GI; 164 (LO RT), Universal Images Group North America LLC/DeAgostini/AL; 165 (CTR), osmar01/age fotostock; 165 (LO LE), Tupungato; 165 (purple gem), PjrStudio; 165 (garnet), PjrStudio; 165 (oval diamond), PjrStudio; **CHAPTER 9:** 166-167, Alberto Ghizzi Panizza; 168-169 (BACKGROUND), Callie Broaddus; 168 (LE), Phitha Tanpairoj/SS; 168 (RT), Fotos593/ SS; 169 (LE), NASA/JPL; 169 (RT), NASA/MSFC/Aaron Kingery; 170 (LE), StagnantLife/SS; 170 (firefly), IamTK/SS; 170 (RT), Doug Perrine/SeaPics.com; 170 (LO), Doug Perrine/Nature Picture Library; 171 (UP), Chien Lee/MP; 171 (LE), NGIC/AL; 171 (RT), Lyu Hu/SS; 171 (LO), Tonywang86/SS; 172-173, Petri jauhiainen/SS; 174 (UP), angelinast/SS; 174 (CTR), Fotosearch/age fotostock; 174 (LO), Aflo Co., Ltd/AL; 175 (UP), sololos/GI; 175 (CTR LE), Larry Landolfi/Science Source; 175 (LO CTR), Foxyliam/SS; 175 (LO RT), Lauritta/SS; 175 (CTR LE), Aflo Co., Ltd./AL; 176, Stocktrek Images, Inc./AL; 177 (UP), Thitisak Mongkonnipat/GI; 177 (CTR), Tropical studio/SS; 177 (LO), sihasakprachumk; 178-179 (BACKGROUND), Gail Johnson/GI; 178 (CTR), Gerry Ellis/MP; 178 (RT), Ethan Daniels/SS; 179 (LE), CSP_jkraft5/age fotostock; 179 (RT), Palladium/age fotostock; 180 (UP), Olga Kashubin/SS; 180 (RT), Mark Kolbe/GI; 180 (LO), katacarix/SS; 181 (UP), Brook Mitchell/GI; 181 (RT), Cameron Spencer/GI; 181 (LE), Cameron Spencer/GI; 181 (LO), katacarix/SS; 182, Stocktrek Images, Inc./AL; 183 (CTR), SS; 183 (UP), Dan Regan/Lick Me I'm Delicious; 183 (RT), Masana Izawa/MP; 183 (LE), Julian Favovich; 184 (BACKGROUND), NASA/GI; 184 (RT), Jurik Peter/SS; 184 (CTR), C. S Jeffery, Armagh Observatory and Planetarium; 185 (LE), ESA/Hubble & NASA/Science Source; 185 (RT), DSS/STScI/ AURA/Pal/Cal/UKSTU/AAO/SS; **BACK MATTER:** 186-192 (diamond picture borders), Mishatc/DS; 192 (UP), Doug Armand/GI; 192 (LO), Universal Images Group North America LLC/DeAgostini/AL

Copyright © 2019 National Geographic Partners, LLC

Published by National Geographic Partners, LLC. All rights reserved. Reproduction of the whole or any part of the contents without written permission from the publisher is prohibited.

Since 1888, the National Geographic Society has funded more than 12,000 research, exploration, and preservation projects around the world. The Society receives funds from National Geographic Partners, LLC, funded in part by your purchase. A portion of the proceeds from this book supports this vital work. To learn more, visit natgeo.com/info.

NATIONAL GEOGRAPHIC and Yellow Border Design are trademarks of the National Geographic Society, used under license.

For more information, visit nationalgeographic.com, call 1-800-647-5463, or write to the following address:

National Geographic Partners
1145 17th Street N.W.
Washington, D.C. 20036-4688 U.S.A.

Visit us online at nationalgeographic.com/books

For librarians and teachers: ngchildrensbooks.org

More for kids from National Geographic: natgeokids.com

National Geographic Kids magazine inspires children to explore their world with fun yet educational articles on animals, science, nature, and more. Using fresh storytelling and amazing photography, *Nat Geo Kids* shows kids ages 6 to 14 the fascinating truth about the world—and why they should care. **kids.nationalgeographic.com/subscribe**

For information about special discounts for bulk purchases, please contact National Geographic Books Special Sales: specialsales@natgeo.com

For rights or permissions inquiries, please contact National Geographic Books Subsidiary Rights: bookrights@natgeo.com

Designed by Julide Dengel

Library of Congress Cataloging-in-Publication Data

Names: Davidson, Rose M., author.
Title: The big book of bling / by Rose Davidson.
Description: Washington, DC : National Geographic Kids, [2019] | Audience: Ages 8-12. | Audience: Grades 4 to 6. | Includes index.
Identifiers: LCCN 2018031316| ISBN 9781426335310 (hardcover) | ISBN 9781426335327 (hardcover)
Subjects: LCSH: Rocks--Juvenile literature. | Gems--Juvenile literature. | Minerals--Juvenile literature. | Crystals--Juvenile literature. | Rocks--Identification--Juvenile literature. | Gems--Identification--Juvenile literature.
Classification: LCC QE432.2 .D38 2019 | DDC 552--dc23
LC record available at https://lccn.loc.gov/2018031316

The publisher would like to thank the following people for making this book possible: Kate Hale, executive editor; Lori Epstein, director of photography; Danny Meldung, photo editor; Jennifer Geddes, fact-checker; Aleks Gulan, design assistant; Molly Reid, production editor; Sally Abbey, managing editor; and Anne LeongSon and Gus Tello, production designers.

Select pages from this book are adapted from the following stories in *National Geographic Kids* magazine:

p. 10-13, Adapted from: Catherine D. Hughes, "Birthstone Myths and Facts," Feb. 2014, pp. 14-17; p. 36-37, Adapted from: Jamie Kiffel-Alech, "The Richest Pets of All Time," Feb. 2017, pp. 22-23; p. 56-57, Adapted from: Jamie Kiffel-Alech, "Lost and Found Treasures," June/July 2014, pp. 22-23; p. 76-77, Adapted from: Becky Baines, "Space Base," February 2016, pp. 22-23; p. 100-101, Adapted from: Scott Elder, "Hot Spot," November 2014, pp. 24-25; p. 176-177, Adapted from: Renee Skelton, "Blue Volcano," March 2015, pp. 22-23

Printed in China
19/PPS/1